Beauty from Ashes

EXPERIENCING PEACE IN
THE MIDST OF LIFE'S STORM

(A MEMOIR)

Petre-Ann Williams

NEW HARBOR PRESS

RAPID CITY, SD

Williams/New Harbor Press
1601 Mt Rushmore Rd, Ste 3288
Rapid City, SD 57701
https://NewHarborPress.com

Ordering Information:
Quantity sales. Special discounts are available on quantity purchases by corporations, associations, and others. For details, contact the "Special Sales Department" at the address above.

Beauty from Ashes / Petre-Ann Williams. -- 1st ed.
ISBN 978-1-63357-254-6

Contents

prologue

Habakkuk 2: 2-3 And the Lord said to me: "Write my answer on a billboard large & clear so that anyone can read it at a glance and rush to tell others. But these things I plan won't happen right away. Slowly, steadily, surely the time approaches when the vision will be fulfilled. If it seems slow, do not despair for all these things will surely come to pass. Just be patient! They will not be overdue a single day."

Why do bad things happen to good people? It's the lottery winning question! Worse yet is seeing "bad" people get away with all that's foul while those that choose to lead a lifestyle more fitting for society's approval struggle. The question is often asked, "what is this life that we should be mindful of it"? What happens when you have been forced to sit, or when life changes in an instant and you can no longer do the things that you once did. What happens when you are laying on a hospital bed staring at the ceiling and ponder, how did I ever get here or when your child is sick, and even when your loved one dies? It's in moments like those that you crumble and learning to breathe again becomes a chore. But, life goes on even when yours has stopped. So let me preface, that I chose to believe in someone greater than or bigger than me. Someone that gives us Free Will, someone who orchestrates time and space. Someone who is fair and just even when bad things happen to good people. Let me also preface, that where there is good, evil is present. Just like you can't have fruits without a tree, or you can't have clouds without a sky you can't really understand what good is until you have experienced what bad looks and feels like. Too often we give Good a Bad name and fail to recognize that Bad has a name also. So, when bad things happen to good people we often lash out and ask God "why did you allow this to happen to me" instead of recognizing that maybe it wasn't God, maybe Evil was present. Evil can only do what it knows and what it knows is nothing good! Church going folks call that Spiritual Warfare. It's the day all "Hell" breaks loose on your life or your loved ones and you can't make sense of why this is happening, especially for the fact that you are a "good" person and it shouldn't be happening to you. But I'm getting ahead of myself......

the beginning

So.... I come from humble beginnings. My story begins in another country. A country I love but was forced to flee with my parents and 2 older siblings at the thought of a possible communistic take over. It is no easy feat leaving everything you know for the unknown. As kids we were care-free, we had friends, we had community, we loved life, we had family. We were suddenly uprooted, and we found ourselves in a land where we knew no one, had no friends nor family, had no community. My parents were hard working people who sold everything they owned in order to afford a one-way ticket to the land of opportunity. My father, who several months prior, had gone ahead of the family to try to secure a place for his wife and 3 children had been blessed to be given a couch at a friend's home to lay his head. He met us at the airport with his friend. With a big hug and uncertain eyes, he greeted us with a smile happy to see his family. "Where are we going daddy", I would innocently ask. "Wherever you want to go" was his simple reply. I remember seeing a highway for the first time in my life. As children we had no idea. The country we migrated from was a 3rd world country at the time and "highways" were foreign to us children. I remember telling my dad I wanted him to drive on the "Big Hill", because as far as I was concerned the Highway resembled a hill and that was my only point of reference. "Drive on the hill" I would yell from the back seat of his friend's car. And consequently, he did and although we got lost on this "hill", looking back it certainly made for great memories. Up until the time we arrived in the United States my dad began attending the church his friend attended. It was there he met an elderly lady (affectionately called Mama G) who willingly opened her home to a man she did not know and his family she had never met. With suitcases in hand we arrived at her home in a strange land, not knowing what to expect. She lived in a humble 2-bedroom house in what we refer to now as "the Hood". My mother drilled into us children's head to always clean up after ourselves, leave every area neat, and be polite even if it's not reciprocated. Mama G slept in her room, my parents in the guest bedroom, and all 3 children on the couch. It was not an easy living arrangement, but we were blessed to have accommodations in this strange land. My brothers being older than me began to pine and weep for what was better times back home. At least there we had our own bed and room. We had friends, we had family and we had community there. Here we had nothing! I remember times where we would sit on Mama G's couch to watch tv. We had become attached to a certain show called "Wrestling" where a character named Dusty Rhodes stole the show. He was a popular wrestler and us kids loved watching him. One particular day as we were screaming with delight that Dusty Rhodes was on the verge of

beating his opponent, we watched Mama G calmly walk over to
the tv and change the channel to her favorite show and sat down
in her rocking chair as if we didn't exist. Our mouths dropped
and our eyes grew wide with anger that she would do such a
thing. I know you saw us watching the tv…. How dare you be so
rude we all thought but couldn't say a word. This was her house,
her couch, her tv, her rules. She could do whatever she wanted
and that she did, as that incident was the first of many more to
come, and our parents quickly reminded us to keep our mouths
shut! Having nothing can be humbling. Since we had no car, my
father would get up early in the morning to walk or catch a bus
to find employment so that he could support his family (and better yet, to get out of Mama G's house). There can only be one
man in a house, and this was NOT his home. Once my father
found employment, I can distinctly remember those days when
my father would make a sandwich to take to work in the mornings for lunch. He would carefully cut his small sandwich in half
and would take half of the sandwich to work to eat today and the
other half to eat for lunch the following day. We were poor but
as kids we just didn't know it. So, my mom registered us for
school. Three kids, three different ages, three different schools.
My eldest brother was in high school, my middle brother was
registered to junior high, and me being the youngest was placed
in elementary. School here in the US was so different from school
in the country of my homeland. Back "home" I was such an
extrovert involved in many activities at school. Here, no one
knew my name and I knew no one. I remember the kids at school
would laugh at me and call me names. They said I spoke "funny"
and because of that I had no friends. I was an outcast. Ironically
enough, I thought they spoke funny, but I didn't say a word (we
both spoke English…but speaking with an accent is speaking

"funny" I guess). When the time came for recess we were dismissed to an open field for free play. This open field was surrounded by a large wire fence which separated the elementary from the junior high school. This one particular day during recess I wondered around on the open field by myself feeling isolated. I sat quietly by the wire fence pulling the weeds from the grass that I thought were flowers simply trying to make myself smile. It was then that I noticed my middle brother on the opposite side of the wire fence. He came over to me and I saw the look of sadness in his eyes. As we spoke to each other through the wire links I softly said, "I want to go home". He knew exactly what I meant…. Home, where we had friends, family, and a community! He looked at me and responded with "I want to go home too". Suddenly our short conversation was interrupted by a loud whistle where the teacher yelled that recess was over and it was time to go back to the classroom. Once school was out, I was informed that I would be taking the school bus home. Now mind you…. In my country we didn't have school buses. This too was foreign to me and no one explained the process. I simply got on a bus (just picked one) with the expectation that it would take me to Mama G's front door. It was the strangest thing, this "school bus" would make periodic stops and groups of children would get out. So, I made the decision that at the next stop I would get out too. I confidently walked off the bus with the next group of students and they went on their merry way. Unfortunately, I hadn't a clue where I was or where I should go. The bus drove off and there I stood at the tender age of 6 like a frightened wet puppy. The houses looked vaguely familiar so in my feeble mind I thought if I would walk long enough, I would eventually find Mama G's house. Five minutes of walking turned into over 2 hours of walking. So, I grew tired and finally sat down on the dirty sidewalk and cried. Night was approaching and I was hungry and lost. Little did I know that my family was out on foot searching and combing the neighborhood for me. Eventually they found me on the same sidewalk and the reunion was filled with pure joy! I couldn't have been any happier to see my family. Ironically enough I was only two blocks away from Mama G's house and had no idea! So close and yet so far. After 3 months of staying at Mama G's house (it seemed like eternity) dad proudly announced one Saturday morning that we were moving. To this day I have no idea how he found this place, which was no where close to Mama G's house, but the idea of having our own home was welcoming. We graduated from sleeping on the couch to having a home with 3 bedrooms and 2 bathrooms. That was even more than we had in our "home" country (which was a 2-bedroom one-bathroom home). It was a modest house on a quiet street. It was a rental with little to no furniture, but it was OUR home. In order to get to work in the mornings, my father was blessed to acquire a car from one of the church families. Mom was forced to find work using public transportation (bus) while dad was at work. That left all 3 kids at home to get into mischief and fights until adult supervision arrived at the end of the day. Mom finally took the time to register us for school and once again, due to our age differences, we were all at 3 different schools. I distinctly remember leading up to our first day of our new school my parents took the time to go over the walking route so that no one would get lost. Because all 3 children where at different schools due to ages/ grade (my big brother in high school, my middle brother in junior high, and me in elementary) it meant different dismissal times and different walking routes. So, my parents came up with an elaborate plan that involved all three siblings meeting up at a specified location after dismissal so that we could all walk home together without anyone getting lost. Since high school was dismissed at 2:30 my eldest brother would walk to a certain location and wait patiently for me who would be dismissed at 3:00. I would then meet him at the location and we would wait for our middle brother who would be dismissed at 3:30. By the time we all found each other and began the LONG walk home it was already after 4:00. To say the least it was the worst plan ever and lasted only for that day. During the course of our walk the conversation went a bit something like this: Big Brother- "This is crazy. I've been standing here since close to 2:30. I can't do this ever again. Does everyone know how to find their way home?" Middle Brother- "Sorry you all had to wait on me". Me- "I can walk home by myself". For a six-year-old I was confident and quite cocky! So, from that day forward we did it our way and never told our parents. Walk on your own, don't get lost, and get home safely! For me the BEST part of the long walk home, besides feeling independent, was that everyday I could see my Big Brother at a distance half way into my walk. I would yell his name LOUDLY to get his attention and he would wait for me to run and get caught up with him. We would then walk the rest of the way home together. Honestly, it was the highlight of my day. Something about seeing a familiar face and hanging with my Big Brother was the greatest (especially when you have no friends). My Elementary years were filled with lots of highs and lows. Somewhere from 2nd grade to 6th grade I went from being a non-entity to everyone knowing my name. It always amazes me how God works. As I mentioned earlier that my faith in something greater, bigger, higher, stronger than me has always been a part of my life. I've often heard it said, "children learn what they live" and my parents lived according to God's word

[handwritten margin notes: "for family members?" and "why we use nemeof 'illustrant' 'pop' person"]

(the Bible). So, I grew up in a Christian household, going to church every Sunday and youth meetings/Bible Study/and prayer meetings all somewhere in between during the week. Elementary was a time of fitting in. It was a time of going to the school playground and being told "you can't play here unless you are wearing "designer jeans""! Designer jeans…. like what's that?! It was a time of proving myself to myself. It was a time of showing others that this little girl from a 3rd-world country was somebody. By the time I entered 6th grade, I had friends, was the Lieutenant of the Safety Patrol, was voted Most Outstanding Athlete by my PE Coach, and received so many notable awards that even the secretaries in the front office knew my name. Junior High quickly approached. Quite honestly…. it was a time of discovering who you are. I was the epitome of health, joined the track team, made lifelong friends, had some great laughs (and many sad moments too), but simply learned what being a teenager was all about. It was a coming of age when boy likes girl and girl likes boy. Feeling the pitter-patter in the depts of your heart when you experience a "crush" for the very first time. His name was Neil. Just your average kid. We were friends in class, no big deal. We spoke, said "hi", laughed at the same silly things…. You know just friends. I would often catch him starring at me. It felt so awkward! When I looked to make sure it was not just my imagination, he would quickly turn his head away, pretending not to stare. But I knew! Outside of school Neil and I would see each other at the neighborhood church. For one week we attended Vacation Bible School (VBS). It was a great alternative from being on the streets. They provided free food, games, arts & crafts, while teaching the neighborhood kids great moral lessons from the Bible. We laughed, played, hung out, and were good friends. I distinctly remember one night at VBS when the

Pastor made an altar call and Neil quietly went up. I was secretly excited for him but didn't say a word. We were taught that this was an outward sign that the individual had accepted Jesus Christ as their personal savior (something I had done at the age of 6 with my parents at my bedside as we prayed together one night before bed). In doing so that individual would have a spot guaranteed in heaven. But the thought of heaven was so far away. We were teenagers, and we were young. Junior High continued to bring about lasting memories. From rushing to your lockers to get your books for the next class to being caught up in a Hall Sweep and trying to avert getting a detention. Neil and I would see each other in passing and wave a quick hello until the next time. The next time couldn't come soon enough. Thanksgiving weekend was quickly approaching. School would be out for the short holiday and then it would be several days before I would see my friends again. It was a Wednesday, we laughed, said our good-byes and Neil winked at me as if to say see you on Monday when we get back. Thanksgiving was great. My parents made an awesome meal and my brothers and I ate our bellies full. On Friday, I went to go hang out at my "Besties" house. The cool part was that she lived only a 20-minute bicycle ride away. In the 80's that's how it was done. Your bicycle was your best friend and took you many places. We hung out and did what teenage girls do, giggle at everything silly, talk about school and boys, and just gossiped! On Saturday, I received a call from my Bestie. She was frantic and the sound of her voice was unnerving. She said many things on the phone all in a rush and a rattle but all I heard was "Neil is dead…. did you hear me, Neil is dead". Now I'm not one for pranks but this was a little over the top. So, I told her to stop playing and there was silence over the phone. For a brief moment I thought IMPOSSIBLE. I just saw Neil 2 days prior as we left school. He couldn't be dead. Death is for the elderly and we are teenagers, we are invincible…. Right? She went on to say that he was hit by a car several houses from her home on the same small street where she lived. I lost it! Honestly, I completely lost it. In the months and years to come following Neil's death I found it hard to sleep, concentrate, and just live. No one knew of my struggle. I kept it to myself. Everyone went on with life while mine had stopped. No one knew of our secret friendship. The most difficult part was going to class and looking over at the empty chair where he once sat waiting for his secret stare that never came back. Oh, how I wept! It was the first time the thought of death ever entered my senses. Before that day I was a carefree teenager with life on my mind. I remember reaching a breaking point. It's amazing how God works. One night I had the strangest dream. I dreamt that I was getting on the school bus preparing to go to school early that morning. As I sat on the school bus while I waited for it to pick up the other students, riding the bus as well, the door opened and Neil walked up the bus steps to get on and take his seat. He didn't say anything to me but smiled as he walked by down the aisle. As he smiled I felt as if I could read his thoughts and it was simply this….. "It is well with me"! I woke up in a cold sweat and wept some more. Somehow, I believe to this very day that was Neil's way of saying from this day forward, cry for me no more. It is well with my soul (and instantly I thought about Vacation Bible School/VBS and the evening Neil went up for the altar call). The death of Neil has been the most life altering event of my junior high years. High school was a transitioning period. We were the last of the 10th grade class coming into high school as the school district was implementing placing 9th graders at the high school level. So, I entered high school not as a Freshman but as a Sophomore and it felt great. High school was some of the best years of my life. It was filled with clubs, and activities, football games, driving to McDonald's for lunch, having my first car, having my first job, Grad Nite, prom, running hurdles on the track team, and a myriad of things to come. It was meeting people that have remained to this very day some of my truest, best, and lifelong friends. I felt blessed to have been voted by my senior classmates Best Personality and also Most Congenial. I still reflect... how does a little girl from a small 3rd world country, who knew no one get to a place where everyone knows your name. And I am convinced that God's hands and the power of praying parents sustains. I wrapped up my senior high years by being blessed to be given the privilege to say the Farewell Speech at my senior graduation. It was the pinnacle of my high school days and to date many have said it was the best graduation speech they have ever heard.

Application: to everything there is a season, a *Beginning* and an end date. Learn to find the beauty in your season. If you don't, life will determine what that looks like for you.

transitions

THE TRANSITION TO COLLEGE life and experiences was not an easy one. Although blessed *thankful* with FREEDOM, it was both a curse and a blessing. I knew nothing about financial aid and was hard pressed for money to pay for school. My dad was out of a job and my mother was burning the candle at both ends in order to provide for the family. My eldest brother was now married and out of the home and my middle brother had just completed college and was at the start of a new career. The financial aide office at school, with much effort, couldn't figure out why I didn't qualify for financial aid. There I was...stuck, desiring to get an education with no money. And so, my side hustle began, working three jobs and going to school full time. It was the only way to pay for my classes. My brothers gave me money to help pay for my books. Quite honestly, sometimes the books themselves cost more than the classes. My mom never veered from her oath: "I've committed to getting you through your bachelor's degree". Hers was a sacrifice beyond words. On a lighter note, college life was fun, exciting, and some of the most memorable years of my life. No one to tell you that you MUST attend classes. No bells ringing to signal a class change. No "hall sweeps", and certainly no detentions for missing classes. It was freedom at its best. But sometimes, freedom can be a curse if not used responsibly. So, I chose not to go to classes and hung out with my friends instead. Big mistake.... I quickly learned that when YOU are paying for your own classes going to class is not an option. After failing my first semester, it never happened again! College came with great campus life, taking free trips on the college's dime, wild parties, great friends, and by far the most fun years of my life. It also came with the dauting reality that racism was very real. Upon leaving campus one afternoon in my vehicle I was startled by the glare of flashing red lights behind my car. I nervously pulled my vehicle to the side thinking that the law enforcement officer was simply trying to get around me in a haste to address the problem. The officer slowed his car, then came to an abrupt stop. He jumped out his police car and approached my window. I had never received a ticket a day in my life and had no idea why I was being pulled over. He then asked to see my identification without even a hint of what I had done wrong, if anything! I nervously asked why I was being pulled over and what I did wrong. He refused to give me an answer. I began to tremble as I was by myself and I had no telling what he was going to do next. He then approached my window once again and told me to open my trunk. I asked why.... And still no answer except "I SAID OPEN THE TRUNK"! What came next still shakes me to this very day. "Where's the drugs.... Show me the drugs". Huh, What?!? I had no idea what he was talking about. I certainly had no drugs. Quite honestly, I was so naïve I couldn't tell you what drugs looked or even smelled like. He continued to strong-arm me. "Where are you hiding the drugs, under your seat or in the trunk of your car? If you don't tell me where in the trunk of the car you are hiding it, I'm calling for back up". At that very moment I KNEW he was going to plant drugs in the trunk of my car. There were no cell phones back then, no way to record what was happening, and no one to call. I was all alone and scared. It would be my words against his and a black female would lose every time. Terrified, I called out to God! All the Sunday School lessons and church sermons I had ever heard came rushing through my head as I silently whispered a prayer.... "Lord, help me"! And He did what He always does, He showed up. The Bible says in James 5:16 *"The effectual fervent prayer of a righteous man availeth much"*. The police officer approached my window once again. I asked "Officer, what did I do wrong, why was I pulled over"? This time, he said nothing about the drugs he claimed I had but stated that I had made a "rolling stop" when leaving the college campus. Although I knew he was lying, I just wanted to be left alone and get back to my family. As I pulled my car slowly away, my hands were trembling, and I cried all the way home. It could have easily ended up differently. Looking back, my college years were just a precursor of things to come, but I would never trade those experiences. My college years taught me resilience, it taught me survival, it taught me hard work and it certainly taught me how to rely on God. This entity I could not see yet I could feel His very presence working for my good even when the situation looked bleak. A "Faith Walk" as the Christian community calls it. I ended my college years earning a bachelor's degree with no scholarships, no grants, and no student loans, poor as dirt…. owing NOTHING and debt free! Isn't God good **(Galatians 6:9 *"And let us not grow weary of doing good, for in due season we will reap, if we do not give up"*)**.

Application: *Transitions* are turning points. Oxford dictionary defines it as "the process or a period of changing from one state or condition to another". Embrace change, whether good, bad, or indifferent, it will come!

changes

THE NEXT STAGE OF my life took me through relationships, heartbreaks, a career and marriage. Leaving college, I was scouted by several schools to be hired as a teacher. My Bachelor's Degree was in the field of Education and during that time, Affirmative Action was huge. Affirmative Action is described as the "practice/policy of favoring individuals belonging to groups known to have been discriminated against previously" (from Oxford Languages). Schools in some of the most affluent areas sought to hire me simply because I was a minority. I conclude that I was highly recruited because of my intelligence, which my grades spoke to, and God's grace. I was blessed to land a job close to home at a public school in a predominantly Jewish area. So here began the journey of being one of the few black teachers at an all Caucasian school in a Jewish community. Truth be told, no one wanted their kid in my class. There were whispers, "she's new, she's young, she's black, she's inexperienced". Once again,

I had to dig deep and prove myself to the masses. In my seven years at that school I went from a virtual unknown to being the teacher with the highest student state test gains in the school every year. I was gifted with the position of Department Head by my Principal (a highly sought-after position by faculty members) and parents were requesting for their child to be placed in my class. As one parent put it "the word is out on the street and the neighborhood is talking about you". God's favor, there's nothing quite like it! As I was educating the students, they in turn were educating me. Before then I knew nothing about Bar Mitzvah's/Bat Mitzvah's and now I was receiving invites to attend such functions. While working full time, I made the decision to go back to school and earn a Master's degree in School Counseling. I would complete my workday by making the long journey to the other side of town to get to class at the University which was over an hour and a half away in the middle of rush hour traffic. My days would begin at 6 a.m. and would end near midnight at least four days a week. One semester I was taking a class entitled "Crisis Counseling". The class would teach you the in's and out's of handling an individual's response to a traumatic event. I didn't know that God in His infinite wisdom would trust me into using what I was learning before its time. But nothing is ever before its time as I would soon learn. My principal had recently hired a teacher's aide to work with me as my classroom was overcrowded with students. At the time I was teaching 45 students in a classroom built for only 30 students at max. The teacher's aide was young, friendly, and a fresh welcomed addition to my classroom. We struck up great conversations and she was very easy to talk to. I had just completed my second class of Crisis Counseling the evening prior when the teacher's aide the next day asked if she could speak to me privately. I thought nothing of it and we struck up a conversation while the student's were at lunch. She began the conversation casually speaking about her stepdad. Her mom had recently gotten married and now her mom's boyfriend was her stepfather. Then the conversation took an eerie turn. She went on to describe how her stepfather would come into her room at nights and rape her. This would take place on several occasions and her spirit was tormented by what he was doing against her will. She confided in me and described in details her plans to kill him that same day as she knew he would enter her room once again to rape her and the gun was set. I sat completely dumbfounded. Was I being pranked? Was this a set-up by some outside source to see how I would handle a "crisis" situation when confronted with it? Was I on a hidden camera? Needless to say, I dug deep to think of everything I had learned over the last two days in my class to help her. I felt so inadequate at her greatest time of need, but God's timing was perfect. Jeremiah 29:11, *"For I know the plans I have for you, declares the Lord, plans for welfare and not for evil, to give you a future and a hope"*. In my last 29 years of teaching I have encountered so many noteworthy events all vying for their stories to be told (that's another book of its own) but that too is still being written.

Application: Whether we admit it or not, our bodies and minds experience *Changes* every day. How we respond to these changes can determine the trajectory of our lives. Learning to seek God in the hush of it all can be deafening. And all too true, the loud clamor can drown out the message He desires us to glean also. It is encouraging to know that God has a plan for each of us. His word is clear that this plan involves a "future and a hope" and is "not for evil". Embrace his plans even when they do not make sense entrusting it to the will of God.

4

waiting

"Wait for the Lord; be strong and let your heart take courage; wait for the Lord", Psalm 27:14.

The next chapter of my life took me through the woes of relationships. Love is a strange exploit. It can consume you, make your heart go "pitter-patter", put you in a state of euphoria. Love is pure, painful, sweet, and dreadful. If you have ever been in love you know the feelings. After experiencing the let downs of being in love and entering a major state of depression I vowed never to allow myself to go back there. It is possible to know someone and not ever really know them. Yesterday he knew my name and today I was a felting thought. I'll never understand that, but God has a way of shutting doors He never intended for us to go through. When you are in love, sometimes your vision becomes clouded and it takes a storm to appreciate the rainbow. Years later, I met my rainbow (my husband) on a blind date. Twenty some odd years, two children, and one grand child later and we are still standing. That's a testament of God's favor. It has not been without its trials, as with all relationships, however, as the scripture says in Philippians 4:6 *"Be anxious for nothing, but in everything by prayer and petition, with thanksgiving, let your requests be made known to God"*. What I could not understand God was working out for my good. And so, I reflect on my single friends who desire to be married and age seems to be gaining on them without a prospect in sight. To them I say do not lose hope, but most importantly don't miss the season you are presently in for the sake of desiring marriage. Marriage is not for the faint at heart. That's why so many people get it wrong and the divorce rate is so high. It's hard work and can either make or break you emotionally. As author Margaret Minnicks puts it "the Bible is quite clear about marriage and remaining single. In order to fulfill one's purpose, the Bible says it is best not to marry. If you continue wanting to be married when God has plans for you to remain single, you will never find real peace as long as you are striving to be married". Probably not what most single folks (especially my single lady friends) want to hear. "I want to have kids.... My biological clock is ticking! I don't want to have kids outside of marriage, but I don't want to get married just to have kids." Everything in its time. What's for you is for you. Your prayers should align with God's will for your life. If you are not praying what God is praying for you ask His wisdom on the matter and if He shuts the door take heed so you don't become a statistic.

Application: I read an article recently with the words "Sometimes God has to wait for His own words to be fulfilled" (excerpt taken from The Hoot & Howl). Why is that so..... because God is at work in the *Waiting*. Please know that your waiting has a purpose, this period of holding and delay is not in vain but working for your good if you have the patients to see it out. In Psalms 27:14, we are reminded that the Lord says to wait on Him and as you wait to take courage but, wait for the Lord. When we realize that we are in control of nothing, it is then we come to the understanding that he sometimes does his best work in the wait!

5

seasons

*"I love the Lord, for he heard my cry for mercy.
Because he turned his ear to me, I will call on
him as long as I live", Psalm 116:1-2*

Some things are too difficult to speak but must be spoken. This season was filled with Infertility, Rape, Homelessness, the death of a parent, broken marriage, and jail. Life becomes real when the headline news is about you, but your name has been withheld. When your loved one is dying right before your very eyes and you are helpless to rescue. When your marriage is breaking under the stress of it all, but you smile to "show face". When you've tried for 10 years to have a child but cannot conceive. When you are responsible for placing someone in prison. When you are forced to place your child in a Homeless shelter. Life becomes very real. This

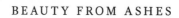

chapter will remain unwritten until its time! Some things are too difficult to speak but must be spoken.... Seasons!

6

signs

"No weapon formed against you will prevail, and you will refute every tongue that accuses you. This is the heritage of the servants of the Lord, and this is their vindication from me declares the Lord", Isaiah 54:17.

Those that know me know my passion for being physically active. On any given day I could be found walking the neighborhood, or jogging the track at the school after work, or even riding my bicycle for miles around the city I live. On the weekends it was with pure pleasure that I would load the back of my truck with balls and bicycles for my son and I to trek and play at the local park. And thus begins my journey that would take me to "hell" and back. Now I don't say that lightly and I give no credence to the dark side. What I do know is that Spiritual Warfare is real and I had just entered it. I entered it unknowingly and it was subtle at first. So, what is Spiritual Warfare you ask? I would describe it as a battle between two forces/spirits that you cannot see over your very soul. It's a war between good and evil over you. Evil wants you and Good fights for you. When your world begins to fall apart and you can't make sense over what is happening, when life changes in an instant and evil seems to be winning you have entered the realm of Spiritual Warfare. The day began like any other. I laced up and placed my exercise gear on after work to jog the track at my place of employment. It was quite convenient and as always, I looked forward to destressing after a long day's work. The students had shuffled out of the building and the track would be peaceful enough for me to jog without the stares of students. My routine consists of 30 laps around the track some jogging but mostly walking all within a certain time frame. The weather was quite warm and I kept a water bottle close by to sip on occasionally so I wouldn't dehydrate in the hot South Florida sun. I excitedly made it around lap 29 and with one more lap to go the end was in sight. Suddenly I realized that something had gone completely wrong. My body began to give out uncontrollably, my heart was palpitating in an unnatural rhythm and I felt as if I couldn't breathe. Everything was spinning around me and I found myself going down slowly. I wasn't sure what was happening, but I knew I needed help and the field was empty. As I staggered towards the grass the lone school custodian, unaware of what was happening, made his way towards the open field to pick up trash as he always did on the golf cart after school. He spotted me collapsed on the grass and quickly made his way over with the cart. He picked me up, placed me on the cart and reached to dial 911 on his cell phone. I softly muttered "don't call 911 call my husband". My husband came immediately as I lived less than 10 minutes from my place of employment. I assured him that I thought my blood sugar may have been a bit low and to simply allow me to lay down and drink some orange juice so my body could regain strength. The next day I decided it was time to call a Cardiologist and make an appointment. I needed peace of mind that everything was okay and wanted assurance that this would never happen again. I decided not to exercise until I got the all clear from the Cardiologist. Several weeks later I saw the Cardiologist who ordered a Stress Test. This involved walking on a treadmill within a certain time frame while increasing the speed of the treadmill and monitoring its effect on my heart. Because I was in top shape, I found this task to be easy and I loved the challenge of it. It allowed me to push myself in front of others and I passed the Stress Test with flying colors. The cardiologist determined that there was nothing wrong with my heart and that my episode on the field several weeks earlier may have simply been an anomaly and it was something to monitor. Over the next year, strange things began happening. I would be playing with my son outdoors, kicking the ball or even riding our bicycles and I would find myself going down as I did a year earlier on the field after work. He was only 10 at the time and I would try my best to stay calm so that he wouldn't be frighten. I remember him looking at me one day at the park when I went down and innocently asking "do you want for me to call daddy"? "No" I would say, but if I can't get up get help from a stranger passing by. Because these episodes were becoming more frequent, I made an appointment with my PCP to seek medical assistance. But once again, they could find nothing wrong and I was told to simply monitor. Several months later I took my bicycle and went for one of my rides around the city. It was a beautiful day and I had already mapped out the route I would take for my ride. It would involve going over a somewhat steep hill, but the views were always amazing. As I made my way up the incline, I immediately knew that something was going wrong. I coasted down the other side of the hill trying to make it to the sidewalk and my body began to give out. Shaking like a leaf I glanced around looking for help. There was no one on the sidewalk. So, I cried out to God. "Lord please help me"! If I can only make it to my friend's home which wasn't too far away, I could get help without being found by a stranger. I got off my bicycle and staggered to the stoplight. I knew my friend was only a few blocks away and I had the will and drive to make it, but my body suddenly gave out on the hot sidewalk and I collapsed. As I went down, I once again felt my heart palpitating, my head spinning, and I couldn't breathe. I reached for my cell phone but didn't have the strength to dial any numbers. My eyes gazed looking for a stranger, someone simply walking by, but there was no one in sight. Suddenly my eyes caught someone on the opposite side of the street. I mustered every ounce of energy to cry out for help, but they could not hear me. Then around the corner came a gentleman walking his dog. As he approached me he said "ma'am do you need for me to call 911"? Pride stopped me and I said "no, call my husband". Tried as he may, my husband could not be reached. He then ran to get water for me and summoned his family members for help. I softly told him I had a friend who lived close by and to call them and tell them where I was so they could come get me. My friend unfortunately wasn't home, but she quickly reminded me of another mutual friend who was even closer and called on my behalf. Within 5 minutes she and her husband came, picked me up off the sidewalk and loaded my bicycle and by limp body into their car and took me home. It was a long night as my body was extremely weak and my heart kept racing. Over the next few weeks, everything seemed back to normal and life went on as usual. In my mind, although alarmed, I had taken every precaution regarding these "abnormalities" but once again my doctor visits yielded nothing but a clean bill of health. Late one Saturday afternoon, I decided to go walking at the school. I felt safe there as the school resource officer lived on the campus as we had developed a great relationship and I knew he always looked out for me whenever I would exercise on campus especially off school hours. I pulled my truck up to the parking lot, took out my water bottle and proceeded to do some laps. My cell phone was inadvertently left inside the truck and the keys were placed on top of the truck. This now being my last lap I thought nothing of bringing those items with me as it would only weigh me down. As I approached the first turn of my last lap, I could tell that this episode which had suddenly come upon me was NOT going to be good. In a split second I glanced towards the truck hoping that I would be able to make it to my cell phone. Five, four, three, two, one...... and I completely collapsed in a small patch of grass on the concrete parking lot. I have no idea how long I was unconscious for. All I knew was that when I finally came to, it was nighttime, and I was still laying on the ground and no one was around once again. I thought it strange that I didn't see the resource office who was always there but most importantly this time I could not get my body to move. With tears streaming down my eyes I called to a power greater than me. "Lord please help me" I prayed. Isaiah 59:1 says *"Surely the arm of the Lord is not too short to save, nor his ear too dull to hear"*. I looked at my truck in the distance and realized I had to find a way to get to it. With no help in sight and in the dark, on my hands and knees, I slowly dragged my lifeless body on the hard road, towards the truck. I knew I would be found dead next to my truck. After what seemed like a lifetime, I made it to the foot of my truck but had no strength to reach my keys which laid on top of the truck. I muttered another prayer..." Lord please help me, I need you". With the will to live I grabbed the running board at the base of the truck and with divine intervention hoisted my limp body towards the hood of my truck to acquire the keys. With my fingertips barely touching the keys, I hooked my pinky finger around the edge of the key and pulled it towards me allowing it to fall to the ground where I was. The next arduous task was now finding the strength to open the truck door with the keys to get to the cell phone. Kneeling on the ground I raised my hand and placed the keys in the lock opening the door. I pulled myself to the seat reaching with all my might feeling for the cell phone. I grabbed it and once again collapsed to the ground thankfully with the phone in hand. I dialed my husband and told him "Come get me". The more I reflect on this particular incident the greater I become aware of God's presence. When I think back to everything that could have possibly gone wrong (the fact that I was unconscious, alone, in the dark, and the school resource officer was no where in sight) I still thank God for everything that went right.

Application: Key verse (Isaiah 54:17), the enemy seeks to destroy, God seeks to restore and spiritual warfare is real. Sometimes, God provides *Signs* as a precursor for things to come. Be aware and be prepared. Just as Jesus refuted the words of the religious leaders of his day when he was challenged, God will speak through you when you rely on him for defense. Weapons will be formed. There will be new weapons formed by the enemy but the child of God who truly relies on God will find themselves strengthened and protected for the daily battles. Every voice that raises up against you will be silenced. These are benefits enjoyed by God's servants. Vindication comes from the Lord. So, hold tight when trials come upon you as they will. God is still in control!

in an instant

"But when I am afraid, I will put my confidence
in you. Yes, I will trust the promises of God"
Psalm 56:3

My 20th wedding anniversary was quickly approaching and for years my husband and I talked about taking a trip to Vegas. We are not gamblers, and we don't like night life but thought it would be different to go somewhere with a little excitement. It was our first trip to Vegas and we were looking forward to it. While at the airport we ran into a friend we hadn't seen in a while who happened to be on the same flight as us. She was headed to Vegas on business and so we exchanged phone numbers with the intentions of linking up once we were settled in our hotel. Once we arrived, we acquired our rental car and went to drop our luggage off at our hotel. The hotel I chose was perfect for us. It was located approximately 20 miles away from "The Strip". It was quiet, in the most beautiful neighbor, on a huge lake that resembled a beach, and the amenities were perfect. We would be in Vegas for 5 days and planned on making the most of our trip. We had two shows booked and lots of sight seeing to do. However, some things we learned the hard way.... Like never go to Vegas in the summer. The heat was horrific with temperatures reaching a scorching 115 degrees and no rain in sight to cool things down. We went places like the Hover Dam and even drove to Mount Charleston (one of the highest peaks on the edge of Vegas). The snow-capped mountain in the heat of the day was enough to cool my over heated body down. Certainly, one of the highlights of my trip. Then the strangest thing began to happen. I noticed that slowly my body began to experience what felt like panic attacks. As we drove throughout Vegas, I frequently had to ask my husband to stop or pull the car over as I felt like everything around me was closing in on me. It made it difficult for me to breathe and the heart palpitations began once again. I thought to myself "No, not here... not now" and tried very hard to dismiss what was obviously coming over me. The feelings got so strong that several nights I simply stayed in my hotel room and had to forgo one of the shows we had booked to see but sent my husband to enjoy it by himself. On the last night of our trip we once again linked up with my girlfriend we had met with at the airport and she gladly gave us the keys to her high rolling hotel suite that was paid for on the company's dime. She had to leave early and didn't want the room to go to waste so we gladly accepted and couldn't believe our eyes. The suite was in one of the most expensive hotels in Vegas. You had to have a special "pass" in order to enter that section of the hotel. This was where Hollywood glamour stayed and, on our way, up to our room we met a few of them in the elevator. Trying not to be star struck we politely said hello and struck up idle conversation. Once we entered our suite, we could not believe our eyes. It was huge and everything was upgraded with the best linens, the best views in Vegas and top-of-the-line EVERYTHING! We had entered hotel heaven! We then took it upon ourselves to go out and fully experience this lavish hotel we were fortunate enough to be staying at. We even sat and had dinner next to some more Hollywood superstars who sat next to us at the table we were eating dinner at while awe-stunned fans and paparazzi clicked their cameras away. It was a great night. Tired and now wee hours into the morning we retreated to our suite when I noticed that my body began giving way. I told my husband…. "something isn't right". My head began to swim, I felt nauseated, my heart began to palpitate once again, and I couldn't move. For a moment I thought that maybe my body's blood sugar had dropped since I was shaking so badly. I told my husband to go down to the lobby and search for some Orange Juice and bring it back to me (hoping that if I was right it would stabilize my blood sugar levels making me feel whole again). He was gone for what seemed like an eternity. I rolled out the bed and fell to the ground. I had no energy to pull myself back up, so I crawled to the bathroom and waited for my husband to come back all along calling out to the one who had rescued me before…. My Lord. "Father…." I prayed, "please don't let me die here". I KNEW if I went to the hospital I would be admitted and would miss our flight which was the next day. I asked the Lord to keep me strong enough to make that flight.

After eternity (or what seemed like it) my husband returned with the orange juice. I quickly drank it and waited for it to do something extra ordinary. He dragged me back to the bed and a hour and a half later I had enough strength to stand and we immediately checked out of the hotel in an effort to make it back to our hotel where our entire luggage was. We had a Red Eye flight the next day and I knew I was very ill. After checking out, I sat in the lobby of our hotel the entire day not moving an inch until it was time to return our rental car. With much prayer I boarded the flight asking God for a miracle. Since it was a Red Eye flight, He granted me my wish by allowing me to sleep the entire flight until we landed at 6 a.m. When we returned home, I immediately took myself to Urgent Care. I was hoping that the doctors would finally diagnose my case, give me a pill and send me home. But to no avail. "We see nothing wrong with you" they stated, and sent me home with instructions to once again follow up with a Cardiologist. I quickly made an appointment to see the cardiologist once again, but the appointment was so far out that I also made an appointment to see my PCP. The following day, still feeling ill and with no real diagnosis I took myself to the Fire Station. Not sure what I was hoping to gain from that, but I had them take my pressure and listened intently to what they would say. The paramedic stated that my blood pressure was a bit elevated and maybe these symptoms I was feeling was due to my age and the possibility that I was pre-menopausal. In my head I dismissed that thought because I "wanted" to think of myself as still being young and being pre-menopausal meant quite the opposite to me. After describing my symptoms to my primary care physician, she quickly called the cardiologist office to expedite my appointment out of concern. The cardiologist rescheduled my appointment to an earlier date and arranged for me to take a Nuclear Stress Test. It was my understanding that this would involve injecting me with substances that would highlight certain areas of my heart and would allow for them to give me a more precise reading and diagnosis as to what might be happening with me. In addition, I would also have to do another treadmill test that they would monitor as well. The entire process would take approximately 4 hours, so I had to prepare accordingly. While I awaited my new appointment, I continued to struggle with the stresses of daily life. Home brought about stresses with my children. Dealing with a teenager is never easy. Dealing with a teenager whose hormones felt like they were on steroids and whose attitude was beyond mere words was trying at best. This compounded the stress in the home and eventually began affecting my marriage. We were at odds with our teenager and at odds with each other. Work was a stress all onto itself. The Evil one (whom I'll refer to as Satan) was busy on the job. I began to discern that I was under a spiritual attack when a fellow co-worker began spewing insults, rumors, and blatant lies about me without reason. This co-worker took these lies to our Boss and even attempted to influence others in believing the lies. Disillusioned and completely stressed about the matter, as it made no sense to me, I consulted the Lord and He revealed that I was being attacked by the Evil one and about to encounter Spiritual Warfare. At the time I thought a simple prayer would dismiss the matter. The Lord always shows up. Why would this be any different? The day of my appointment for my Nuclear Stress Test, as I prepared to leave work early, I decided to extend an "olive branch" to one of the recipients of this co-worker's lies. I wanted to set the record straight as my good name was on the line, and my reputation was my character and that meant its weight in gold. As I approached this individual, I expressed that I wanted to have lunch and fellowship with them the following day. They agreed and I stepped out the building to hurry off to my appointment with the cardiologist. On my way to the cardiologist I received a phone call from a friend. They were semi aware of my health battles and I shared with them that I was on my way to once again meet with the doctor in hopes that this test would reveal the nature of my aliments. We spoke and laughed and then I made a comment in jest that would continue to haunt me to this very day. I said to my friend on the phone "wouldn't it be funny if I had an episode and the doctors could finally see everything I've been talking about". But we know how that goes... the symptom rarely ever present themselves when you need it to and when you don't it's like a thorn at your side. We said our good-bye's and I proceeded to park my vehicle. Feeling uneasy and nervous I went into the cardiologist office just wanting to get this test over. The cardiologist office was located inside the hospital building which meant I was already tired from walking all the way from the parking lot to the 5th floor where the office was located. I sat waiting for my name to be called. While I waited, I received a call from my daughter. We had idle conversation and then I was called in to get the IV started. Once over that hump I patiently waited for the IV to do its job. I reflected on the day's events up to that moment. Although stressed I was glad to have extended the olive branch to my co worker and was looking forward to lunch the next day. I was also pleased to hear from my daughter as she rarely called and our relationship had been a bit bumpy in recent weeks. The doctor entered the room and proceeded with the first half of the test. He looked at the monitor as the dye from the IV spread to my heart. He mumbled that everything looked great and then told me to sit in the waiting room for the next half of the test. While waiting, I suddenly began to feel nervous and alone. I did something next that I've never done prior.... I called my mother who was away on vacation just to hear her voice. Yes, I've spoken to my mother a million times before, however, I've never called her from a doctor's office, and felt compelled to tell her I love her. Unfortunately, I didn't get her but left a voicemail message expressing my love to her and letting her know that I was scared and wishing she was here with me. I was finally called in for the last portion of the test. This involved the treadmill. I was quite familiar with this portion of the test having done it before and got on the treadmill like a champ. I was definitely in shape and knew I would once again pass this portion of the test with flying colors. The test went well. I got to full capacity on the treadmill and now my Nuclear Stress Test was completed. I got off the treadmill looked at the doctor and nurse in the room and stated, "I don't feel good, I'm about to go down". Little did I know that those were my dying words, and in an instance my life would forever be changed. I don't know what happened next. I do remember barely opening my eyes and all I saw were a team of doctors and paramedics working on my lifeless body. I had no idea where I was. For a moment I tried with all my will to process what was happening. I remember one of the paramedics asking, "Do you know your name"? The next question thrown at me was "Can you tell me what year it is"? I opened my mouth to speak but couldn't process nor form the words to answer their questions. They were pumping on my chest and IV's were everywhere. I recall my cardiologist saying, "We need a number for your husband... can you give me a number"? It's funny how the brain works. I couldn't remember anything else, but I did rattle off my husband's number. The paramedics rolled me out of the doctor's office and into the Emergency Room. I remember sweating and feeling extremely hot. My eyes were closed and I wanted to tell the paramedics that I felt hot but couldn't form the words. And then as if he had read my mind, I heard him say to his fellow paramedic.... "She looks hot and is sweating all over, quick unbutton her and cool her down". When I got to the Emergency Room a team of doctor's were waiting for me. I still had no idea what had occurred and why I was even there. I was in a complete daze, could barely open my eyes, but was taking everything in with my ears. I've heard that the hearing on a dying individual is usually the last thing to go. I remember one of the doctor's shaking my lifeless body asking.... "Do you know where you are and who the president is"? Again, I forced my brain to process and answer the question, but my lips weren't cooperating with me. Tried as I could it was difficult to form the answer on my lips. After 10 minutes of trying I uttered the name of the president but by then I don't think anyone heard me. I cracked opened one eye and saw several IV's hooked up to both arms and my husband speaking with the doctor. Then I glanced around and saw my son sitting on a chair playing with my cell phone. Then I heard the doctors tell my husband that it wasn't good. Apparently when I stepped off the treadmill and uttered those words I immediately went into Cardiac Arrest (supraventricular tachycardia) dropped dead on the floor and lost my life. I later came to find out that my heart rate stepping off the treadmill went up to over 300 beats per minute in an instant. My words of "wouldn't it be funny if I had an episode and the doctors could finally see everything I've been talking about" that I uttered to my friend on the phone had become a reality in the worse possible way. After running a few tests, they also determined that my potassium levels were extremely low and I was whisked away to ICU.

Application: Key verse (Psalm 56:3), we all become afraid of something and life can change *In An Instant*. As you experience your trials put your confidence in the Lord. Regardless of the outcome, He is still in control even when things look bleak. When you become fearful call on him and trust His promises. The phrase "fear not" is used in the Bible at least 80 times. That's not by coincidence, it's a command! So, Fear Not and trust God. His promises are true and his mercies are new every day.

things fall apart

"Do not fear, for I am with you; do not be dismayed, for I am your God. I will strengthen you and help you; I will uphold you with my righteous right hand", Isaiah 41:10

*B*eing in ICU is humbling. You do nothing for yourself! I felt I had enough strength to go to the restroom. You do nothing for yourself. I wanted to wash the sweat off my face. You do nothing for yourself. With the urgency to use the restroom a bed pan was placed under me. This was new territory for me and at first, I was embarrassed. I felt exposed. I told the nurse I think I can make it and she stated that I was not allowed. Someone came in to bathe me on the hospital bed. I felt exposed again. I needed to have a bowel movement. The bed pan was placed under me. This was humbling. I did nothing for myself. A series of events took place with my stay in ICU over the next several days. I was given a cardiac catherization (a procedure in which a long tube is inserted in an artery/vein in my arm and threaded through the blood vessels to my heart) to check for blockage in my heart. Everything came up all clear! I began to complain to my ICU nurse that I was experiencing excruciating pain in my upper left arm. I told her that the pain was unbearable and felt as if it was getting worse. Morphine was given to me and they proceeded to conduct an ultrasound on the arm which later determined that I had a blood clot in my arm. Yes.... Things fall apart! The doctors later shared with my family that they thought it best to implant a defibrillator as a preventative measure in the event that I should ever pass out again. This would entail immediate surgery and would involve me having to be transferred to another hospital for surgery. I couldn't process what I was being told. In my mind I was still the epitome of great health, how could life change in an instant when I did everything to keep myself healthy and fit over the years. After several days in ICU an ambulance was sent to the hospital to transfer me to the Regional hospital for surgery. I was scared, nervous, and crying out to my Lord. When I got to the Regional hospital, I was placed in a room that resembled the size of a small closet which looked like it was never cleaned. Dirty clothes laid on the floor and my roommate was screaming and couldn't help herself. No one came in to assist. I recall laying on the bed awaiting my heart MRI prior to surgery and with tears streaming from my face. I begged the Lord to "Let this cup pass from me". And in a LOUD voice He responded (I heard Him clearly) .... "this cup you will have to partake of", and I wept bitterly! With tears streaming from my

46

face the orderly walked into the room to wheel me away for my test and at that very moment my phone rang. It was a fellow co-worker. She said, "I felt compelled to call you and pray for you. I don't know what's going on with you presently, but the Lord said to pray for you". As she prayed a peace that I cannot explain swept over me. *"And the peace of God, which surpasses all understanding will guard your hearts and your minds in Christ Jesus" Philippians 4:7.*

Application: Key verse (Isaiah 41:10), when *Things Fall Apart* what is your solace? Again, we are being commanded not to fear. Why should we not fear... because God says He is with us. Just think, the creator of this universe knows your name and is with you. So, don't be dismayed as one reacts when in a state of danger. Rest in the assurance that you are being protected by the God of heaven who has all power. He will give you the strength to bear your trials and hold you secure with his mighty hand. And if fear stills seems to be winning, take a deep breath and invite the Holy Spirit to dwell in you and grant you peace.

premonition

"Surely the arm of the Lord is not too short to save, nor his ear too dull to hear", Isaiah 59:1.

was told that surgery went smoothly. The last thing I remembered prior to being placed on the table was the nurse prepping me for what was to come. She scrubbed me down and begin marking my body for where the surgery would be taking place for the doctors. I remember looking down and asking her as to why she was marking my foot for surgery that would be taking place in my heart. She apologized profusely, and was marking me for the wrong surgery. To this day I thank the Lord that I was conscious enough to point out her mistake. It could have been quite costly. I now have a better understanding as to how doctors amputate the wrong leg in a surgery. A pretty scary thought. I couldn't leave that hospital soon enough! Recovery was tough. My chest felt like it had a boulder implanted in it. For days I couldn't move nor lift my left arm, on the side of the chest, where the defibrillator had been placed. Reality once again hits when I (out of pure habit) without thinking reached over to grab the cup of juice on the table next to me with my left arm and realized that I couldn't reach it. Another humbling moment. I cried. I was out of work for months. During that time, I learned how to live again. Fear of exercise and simply walking took me to a whole new level of trust in the God I believed in. If He promised *"never to leave nor forsake me"* why was I in this present predicament? I purposed to trust Him and take Him at His words, and he chose to bring me to new heights in Him. But this did not happen overnight. I went from sitting to standing, from standing to a small walk around my cul-de-sac, and eventually from the cul-de-sac to rounds around my block. I went from having my driver's license withheld to being able to drive again. After months of recovery at home and many doctor's appointments I was back to work 6 months after my incident. I asked the Lord to afford me the opportunity to share my experience with others so that they would not be alone in their journey. Many have asked what I felt or experience at the time of my death. I clearly remember during my hospital stay a mysterious lady walked into my room. I hadn't a clue who she was nor did she know me. But she introduced herself by stating the following "I know you don't know who I am. I saw your case file and I've always been curious about near death experiences. What did you see when you crossed over to the other side"? This is something I rarely speak about, however I felt compelled to respond. And my answer was such.... "I was at complete peace". She smiled, and as mysteriously as she entered, she left never to be seen again. At work, it felt great to be back to some sense of normalcy. Things had changed as I was no longer working out after work or doing all the extras I once did for the sake of "resume" building. That co worker and I never had the pleasure of having lunch as they avoided me like a plague. I was told that they felt semi responsible for my health issues due to the unnecessary stressed they caused. It took a lot of soul searching but God impressed upon me that in order for me to heal I had to forgive them. That's never easy, especially when you are looking for an apology, but the Lord reminded me *"As the Lord has forgiven you, so you also must forgive' Colossians 3:13* and so I did! The school year came to a quick close and summer rolled around faster than I antici-pated. It was filled with excitement and lots of heartaches. My family and I did our usual summer road trip. We always drove to Alabama to visit my husband's family that lived there. As we drove, I noticed the panic attacks slowly coming back. I quickly dismissed it in an effort to enjoy new life. Since my health inci-dent, I had been placed on Beta Blockers (a medication which helps to regulate the heart rhythms and stabilize blood pres-sure). Unfortunately, my body was not acclimating to the Beta Blockers easily and the doctors were forced to change the Beta Blockers on several occasions to finding the right fit for me. While in Alabama on vacation, I also noticed that my heart was fluttering in a manner that was not "normal". On the 4th of July on vacation I ended up in the Emergency room once again out of fear that something had gone awry with my heart. The doctors at the hospital could not find the issue and sent me to a cardiologist the following day after being released from the hospital. I was distraught that my vacation had turned into a nightmare. Upon our return a week later, I made an additional appointment with my cardiologist to follow up. He too couldn't find the issue and made the daunting decision to slowly wean me off the Beta Blockers until we could find a better alternative. This would prove later to be life altering! Summer was coming to a quick close and my family decided to wrap things up with a huge surprise 80th birthday celebration for my mother, and a family vacation and reunion like none other. We rented a huge beach house in Siesta Key, Fl and my siblings and I with their families under one roof simply fellowshipped. While enjoying this time with family, once again I could tell that something was wrong. My body began giving way and I had a difficult time breathing. Walking was an effort and I struggled to climb the stairs in the house. When I mentioned to my family how I was feeling many thought it was in my head and that I was allowing my thoughts to overrule my mind. This was frustrating as I knew my body and I knew something was awry and felt as if I wasn't being heard. One night as I sat on the balcony overlooking the beach, I had a premonition that what was to come was going to be worse than before. I whispered to the Lord to take control and calm my spirit. After a few days with family, vacation ended and we all went our separate ways. I was coming home to an empty house as my husband and son were on their way to North Carolina. That Saturday I was the keynote speaker at a Woman's Conference, and I had the pleasure of sharing with the ladies how the Lord had brought me back from death itself and continues to write my story. Still not feeling too well and knowing I would be alone at home, I contacted my next door neighbor and politely asked her to periodically check in on me. I went to work that Monday and had a pretty good workday. My sister in law called to see how I was feeling and I expressed to her that I wasn't feeling 100% but was looking forward to getting home and laying down. I left work and made a quick stop at the gas station. While at the gas station my body began feeling "weird". I hopped into my car and proceeded to make another quick stop at the store, however, made a U-turn and walked away from the store because my body was telling on me. I couldn't get home soon enough. Once home I made the decision to make dinner early and began cooking at the stove. Suddenly, things went from bad to worse. In an instant my mind said...."turn the stove off and go get help". My heart was beating erratically, and I knew that something was deathly wrong. I looked around for my cell phone to call for help but realized that it was in my purse near the front door. I moved swiftly towards my purse and grabbed my cell phone. As I scrolled to find my sister in law's number my breathing became more labored. She answered and said "Hello" .... and I responded with "Donna, I don't feel good, I need your help". Before I could get the next sentence out of my mouth my body collapsed, and the breath of life left my body. This is difficult to write..........

Application: Key verse (Isaiah 59:1), listen to your instincts. They are subtle hints that something may be awry. I've often heard that God speaks to his children through their conscience, that pause (even for a quick second), to simply question the decision you are about to make. That foreboding thought that danger is near is God's way of telling you to pray. As soon as something grabs your attention, talk to God about it. His hands aren't too short to save you and his ears are bionic. They hear, have heard, and will hear everything uttered under the sun. This includes your cries and secret prayers. Your *Premonitions* are an invitation to pray!

things fall apart some more

"The Lord will fight for you; you need only to be still", Exodus 14:14.

*A*s I hit the ground a bolt of lighting struck my body. I didn't know at first what had occurred. The cell phone flew out of my hands. My earrings flew out of my ears and my entire body flew back several feet. That's when I realized my defibrillator had deployed. It was the most excruciating pain I had ever felt and I couldn't control it. I was too weak to reach the cell phone on the ground but began screaming "Donna, if you can hear me call 911". Immediately the defibrillator went off again and threw me back several more feet. I stumbled to get to my feet trying to make it to the front door so I could summons help, but the defibrillator went off once more and threw me back again. In pure panic and anguish I called for help, but no one heard me.

I was alone inside my house with a locked front door and no way out. I began crawling towards the front door on my hands and knees and as I approached the front door, the defibrillator deployed once again throwing me backwards. I screamed "Lord be merciful to me". I had to find a way outside and my cell phone was now missing. With no energy left in my body, I reached towards the lock on the front door and turned it to unlock the door. Then with every ounce of energy left in my being I pushed the door open but couldn't move. I laid on the ground between the front door and my foyer scanning the sidewalk for someone.... Anyone. I needed help! There were no pedestrians that day. While I laid there dying, the defibrillator went off again and I knew this was the day I would meet my Maker. I began thinking, how would I be found. My family is out of town and isn't due back for several days. Would they come home to a decaying body. On my hands and knees, I began to crawl on my cemented walkway. The hedges leading up to my front door were pretty high so I knew no one could see me on the ground. At this point my body could move no more and I laid face down on the hot cemented walkway waiting for the Lord to take me. As I waited, the defibrillator went off once again. I tried yelling for help but only a whisper emerged. No one was around to hear my cries. Suddenly my neighbor's husband appeared out of nowhere. It's funny how the Lord works but He is always on time! My neighbor had just stopped by his home to pick his wife up. He shouldn't have been there he later stated. His quick stop home was all per chance. He got out his car and thought he had heard a faint cry for help but saw no one. As he was making his way to his home he paused and heard the cries again. He glanced at my house and noticed the front door opened but saw no one and thought it strange. We had been neighbors long enough and he knew I would never leave my front door wide open. He decided to check and make sure I was okay and that's when he discovered me on the ground between the hedges out of sight. With tears in my eyes, I uttered "call 911". He scrambled to lift me up and the defibrillator went off again. There was nothing left in me. He dragged my lifeless body to the couch in my home and called 911. As we awaited 911's arrival the defibrillator went off once more. He yelled for his wife who was a nurse and told her to get to my house immediately. She came and held my hands and while speaking with the 911 dispatchers his phone went dead (no battery life). I whispered to my neighbor's wife "don't get too close, you will get shocked". Fortunately, he was able to give the dispatchers my address before the phone went dead. I told him to find my cell phone which was laying on the floor somewhere in my living room. As we awaited the ambulance's arrival, the defibrillator went off an additional three more times. The only way to describe the pain and pure anguish that comes from being shocked by a defibrillator is to think of a lighting bolt striking you from the inside out. The power is so strong it can cause your body to fly in several directions. I felt like I had been kicked in the chest by a horse. I realized its strength when it blew my earrings (which were latched) completely off my ears before blowing my body several feet. The paramedics arrived and quickly loaded me onto the gurney. I told my neighbor to grab my purse, cell phone and house keys and lock my door. My neighbor's wife came with me in the ambulance since I had no one. The paramedics proceeded to ask me what had occurred. I tried to tell them that my defibrillator had deployed 11 times, but they refused to believe me and asked me to repeat myself thinking I had stated that in error. "11 times", I said "11 times"! They were still in disbelief. When I got to the hospital a team of doctor's awaited my arrival. Deja vu, I thought... I've been here before.

Application: Key verse (Exodus 14:14), the Bible states "if God is for you, who can be against you", the answer is no one. Exodus 14 verse 14 is a reminder that sometimes we have to get out of God's way and simply surrender. When *Things Fall Apart (some more)* being "still" is very difficult to do because it is relinquishing the right to be in control. Instead of fighting yourself, it becomes a waiting on God and observing what he tells you to do. The children of Israel saw no way out and was forced to look up. It was in their waiting that God delivered them. For you it may be a difficult marriage, sickness, or even a wayward child that God has endowed on you. Just remember he will also provide a way out. "The Lord will fight for you, you need only to be still" Exodus 14:14.

it is dark

"Be still and know that I am God", Psalm 46:10.

After my arrival the doctors in the ER worked tirelessly to get the defibrillator under control. Unfortunately, my heart rate continued to rise. Outside the curtains of the ER my neighbor and my sister in law watched nervously. My neighbor was able to get in touch with my sister in law who met her at the hospital. The doctor tried to prepare me for what was to come next. Quite honestly, nothing prepared me for that experience. After applying several IV's, he stated that he would have to stop my heart in an effort to restart it so that they could get my heart rate regulated once again. He explained that the feeling would not be pleasant but that he would hold my hand. As he injected the IV, I silently braced myself for what was to come next. I remember thinking "I don't want to die with my eyes opened" so I made a conscious decision to close my eyes. As the medicine spread throughout my body, it made my body feel hot all over. Then suddenly, I knew my heart had stopped and I was once again in the land of the dead! With my eyes already closed I could see everything that was taking place outside and around my dead body. It was an out of body experience like none other. I saw one doctor looking at the monitor while another watched me intently. Then the doctor that was holding my hands began to say "It's coming down, it's coming down.... Her heart rate is coming down". Then he proceeded to inject me with more medication to bring me back. It's as if I felt my soul reenter my body. I slowly opened my eyes and wanted to tell my story of what I had just experienced. But there was no time for that as the doctor's began to scramble once again. "Her heart rate is going back up; we have to stop it". He looked into my scared eyes and said, "I'm sorry, we'll have to do this again". He held my hands once more and injected me with medication to stop my heart again. The experience was surreal. My defibrillator was turned off and now the doctors were controlling my heart. In the depts of my mind I cried out "Jesus, Jesus, Jesus...... Jesus"! He heard my cry. Once the heart was stabilized, I was then rushed off for a scan and then moved into ICU. I spent several days in ICU and was quite familiar with the process from before. It was humbling once again! My first night in ICU a young man stood out my curtain. He eventually walked in unannounced to my room and simply asked "Have you seen a Bible here"? I looked around with my eyes and said... "I see no Bible". He asked if I would mind if he looked around the room for a Bible. He opened the drawer next to my bedside and I heard him say "There it is" and he removed the Bible from the bed stand. He then looked me in the eyes and said, "My grandma died in this room last night and I know she had left her Bible here and I had to come get it". Not quite what I wanted to hear. I was spooked the rest of my nights in that ICU bed. Anything that creaked or moved I thought about that young man's grandmother. Eventually I was moved from ICU onto another floor in the hospital. The doctors were still at a lost for what caused my 2nd episode and yet they still had no diagnosis for my first episode 10 months earlier. Being in the hospital gives you a lot of time to think. Sometimes that can be a good thing and other times maybe not so good. My husband was notified and he and my son booked a flight to return from North Carolina. As I awaited his return my mother drove in from out of town where she lived to be by my bedside. My son was in North Carolina to participate in the National Junior Olympics competition for Track and Field. He was 11 years old and had qualified for 3 events (the 800, the 1500-meter race and the high jump). It was my intentions to watch him compete from my hospital bed on the computer. I was his biggest fan and my desire was to be with him, but I couldn't. On the day of his competition I was so ill in the hospital that I couldn't watch his race. I kept telling the doctor's as they did their rounds that the medication they were giving me was making me feel very ill and causing my heart to palpitate irregularly once again. One evening it got so bad that the doctors had to rush to my bedside after I pressed the button for help. They were at a lost as no one could diagnose my case. Several days later my husband arrived and never left my bedside. One Sunday morning my husband looked at me and said "I'll be back... I'm going to church". Church was less than 10 minutes from the hospital. I told him to hurry back. Shortly after he left, I received a phone call from a girlfriend of mine in North Carolina. She stated that she called to pray with me on the phone as I laid in the hospital bed. She prayed with me and I felt a sense of relief knowing that I was being prayed for. Still feeling weak a janitor walked into the room. I asked her if she could assist me to the sink to brush my teeth. She helped me up and I made my way over to the sink. As I rinsed my mouth out, I looked up at her and said, "something is about to go horribly wrong" and in an instant the defibrillator went off and threw me backwards. The janitor began to scream not knowing what was happening. As I tried to gain some balance, I yelled "my defibrillator is going off" and it went off once again. She grabbed me and pulled me onto the bed and began pressing the buttons for help. As she did that, the defibrillator went off once more. Frantic... she ran out the room to get assistance. The defibrillator deployed for the final time. As the Lord would have it, all of the hospital's top cardiologist were in the room next door to me seeing another patient when they all rushed in. I could hear on the loud hospital speaker a Code Blue being called. It was for me! After they worked tirelessly to get me stabilized once again, I had completely lost my mind. This was Spiritual Warfare at its best. Someone wanted me dead, and someone wanted me very much alive. I was moved right back to ICU. My husband would later tell me that he received a call from the hospital while at church. They said "come quickly" without an explanation. He arrived with a panicked look on his face. The stress was too much. The decision was then made by the doctors that they would have to once again relocate me back to the Regional hospital. After much discussion, they had a probable diagnosis, however, it would require surgery and for that I would need to be relocated. An ambulance was sent to the hospital to pick me up and I was then transfer back to the same hospital that did my previous surgery. The first inclination that things weren't going to be smooth sailing was prior to my departure they had to reinsert my IV. The issue was, I had been stuck so many times during my stay at the hospital that it was becoming increasing difficult to find my veins. Have I mentioned that I have a HUGE needle phobia? After being stuck several more times in an effort to find my veins, emotionally I was drained. They secured the new IV and off I went with the paramedic. Once I arrived at the Regional hospital the new attending nurse took one look at my IV and stated "No, this needle is too small. You will need a new IV". I pleaded with her letting her know that this one had just been inserted less than an hour prior, but it fell on deaf ears. I cried some more.

Application: Key verse (Psalms 46:10), being still can sometimes be the hardest thing to do especially when your whole being tells you to move. How do you stop fighting and relax when your world is upside down and *It is Dark*? It begins when you acknowledge the fact that the Divine Protector himself is speaking to you. In the verse he not only reminds you of who he is, but that he is God alone. It is a command! So, in knowing that the, "being still" becomes bearable because the outcome will bring glory to his name. He wants you to KNOW that he is in control regardless of what the situation looks like.

heroes

"The Lord himself goes before you and will be
with you; He will never leave you nor forsake
you. Do not be afraid; do not be discouraged",
Deuteronomy 31:8.

My stay at the Regional hospital was much better than before. God had placed me on the exact floor of the cardiac ward that my best friend worked. She chose my room carefully so that as she sat at her desk, she could see me directly. She assigned the very best nurses to my care. Surgery I was told was successful. It ran approximately 6 hours and when I came to my family surrounded me. Unfortunately, the room I was placed in had a dementia patient next to me who screamed the entire night and throughout the day. My girlfriend apologized and moved me several rooms down. Finally, I had my own private room.

Once again, I couldn't stand or walk. It brought me to tears. As I sat in the bed having the urge to go to the restroom a female janitor walked into my room. I asked her if she would help me to the restroom. She was off her shift and was simply walking by to say goodbye as we had developed a relationship during my stay. She took the Walker and assisted me to the restroom. I was so afraid I begged her not to leave me. I knew she had to get home to pick up her grandchildren, but she held my hand for the half hour I sat on that toilet unable to have a bowel movement and didn't complain once. The things we sometimes take for granted. I was losing my mind.

Application: Key verse (Deuteronomy 31:8) this verse speaks to the very nature of God's heart. At times we feel as if God has forsaken us but the fact is that he never will. God wants to help us see Him as he really is and knowing that he goes before us means that he is with us. So, when you become afraid or even discouraged rest in the assurance that because he directs our path the outcome always belongs to him. He is the true *Hero*!

ptsd is real

"We demolish arguments and every pretension that sets itself up against the knowledge of God, and we take captive every thought to make it obedient to Christ", 2 Corinthians 10:5

PTSD is REAL! I had read all about it when getting my counseling degree. I have seen people on tv talk about and even play the role but until you have actually experienced it no words can truly describe it. Not only was I losing my mind, I had completely lost my mind. I couldn't sleep at nights, I couldn't be alone, I was waking up in cold sweats. I had vivid nightmares and flashbacks of what had taken place in my home. As a result, I had panic attacks and my anxiety caused my blood pressure to skyrocket. Everything was a trigger. I remember coming home from the hospital and walking up to my front door. I had flashbacks of me laying on the cement crying out for help waiting to die. I stepped in my home and I could still see the cell phone I couldn't reach under the couch (it was in my mind). This is where I lost consciousness before the defibrillator deployed. Next, I walked into my kitchen and I could still picture the meal I was cooking at the time I began to feel sick when I turned off the stove. Everything was a trigger for me. I sat on the couch in my family room. It was a rainy day and it began to thunder and lightening filled the sky. I screamed....as the lighting brought images of my defibrillator going off in my head. This went on for weeks.... Months! I couldn't be alone. I was afraid to stay inside my home. I was afraid to go outside. I refused to drive. What if I had another episode? What if something were to happen? When the bulb blew on my bathroom mirror the flash from it caused images of my defibrillator to cripple my mind and I screamed in terror. I can't live like this! I couldn't even walk through the living room of my home. I avoided it like a plague. Too many memories. The flashbacks and anxiety would cause my heart to race and palpitate. I would then begin to think that I was having another episode and would lose it once again. I am the strongest person I know but suddenly I became weak and no longer began to recognize myself. PTSD is REAL! Since I couldn't be left alone, my husband each morning on his way to work would drop me by my sister in laws house to be baby sat. She never complained but I felt guilty over something I couldn't control. What had I become? Not a day went by that I didn't cry and cried some more. In an effort not to exhaust my sister in law I began going to work with my husband. He would bring a cot to his job and hide the cot in his office between two boxes so that I could lay down without being seen. This went on for months. I decided to finally go and see a counselor. Imagine, the counselor seeing a counselor. Another humbling experience. It took three tries before finding the RIGHT counselor for me. As well intended as they may be, the fit wasn't right but the 3rd was the charm. The battle of the mind continues but has been made a lot easier once I asked God to take control of my mind and make it obedient to Him. That's huge! I was relying on a source and power greater than myself. That's faith in practice and there is certainly peace in God's presence. The Bible speaks of a "peace that surpasses all understanding" that only God can give. That's where I choose to rest; *"And the peace of God, which surpasses all understanding, will guard your hearts and minds through Christ Jesus"*, *Philippians 4:7.*

Application: Key Verse (2 Corinthians 10:5), whether you realize it or not we are engaged in spiritual warfare. Satan desires our mind and our flesh is powerless against the wiles of the devil. That's why God's word must be our weapon. The wisdom of the wise is destroyed by God. It must be brought under His submission. So, when Satan whispers into your ears and gets a foothold into your mind, cry out to God and ask him to take captive your thoughts/mind and that it would yield to Him. *PTSD* becomes no match for the King of Kings and Lord of Lords. Remember, it takes spirit to fight spirit and only the Holy Spirit can break the strongholds that has you in bondage.

warfare

"For our struggle is not against flesh and blood, but against the rulers, against the authorities, against the powers of this dark world and against the spiritual forces of evil in the heavenly realms", Ephesians 6:12.

Sometimes things fall apart. You take two steps forward and three steps backwards and feel like you can't keep your head above the waves. I continued to cry out to God for his mercy and although I knew He was sustaining me, my season didn't stop and the warfare continued. I received a daunting call from the cardiologist office that the scan of my heart also showed spots on my liver. More hospital scans showed that these lesions on the liver needed to be addressed. The cardiologist went on to explain that they believed I had a rare auto immune disease called Cardiac

Sarcoidosis. They believed that my heart was inflamed, and the disease was causing issues elsewhere in my body. Although there is no cure for this disease treatment would help to reduce the discomfort in the heart. Unfortunately, treatment could not proceed without first addressing the issue of the liver. This would entail getting a biopsy of the liver, and seeing the results. For a split moment I thought .... "What was then the purpose of going through a 6-hour heart surgery? Wasn't that supposed to be the cure"? I distinctly remember the look on the cardiologist face when her words pierced me like a dagger. She said "Life as you know it will never be the same again. You have a long road ahead of you". I left her office with tears running down my cheeks and snot running out my nose. My hope had been sapped and when you have no hope, you have nothing! On the same day that I received this news regarding the need for a biopsy on my liver I also received a call from my gynecologist office. "We've found some cysts on your ovaries that need to be addressed". I thanked them for the call and began to pinch myself. This can't be real. Too much for one person to handle. My girlfriend flew into town to be by my side as I went in to have my biopsy. I was scared beyond words especially not knowing what the results would yield. When the results came back the pathologist were unable to give a conclusive diagnosis, so the report was sent off for a second opinion to the Mayo Clinic in Minnesota. Waiting can be difficult. A thousand things flood your mind. You try to think happy thoughts but "What if it's cancer" slips into your thoughts. Lord, take captive my thoughts and help me to trust you in this season became the cries of my prayers. Things continued to fall apart. I received a call from my son's school. He had injured himself and couldn't walk. They needed me to come get him. Since I wasn't driving at the time (fighting the fears in my mind) I asked my neighbor if she would kindly take me to his school to pick him up. We went from his school straight to the orthopedics' office. I could tell that he had refractured his ankle (for the 3rd time in 3 years) and would need a cast. It's amazing how on time God is. Still having difficulty breathing and experiencing pains in my left shoulder and arm that I could no longer lift (later diagnosed as Frozen Shoulder) I took my son out of the car and pondered, how am I going to get him into the building to see the doctor? He was standing on one leg and I didn't have the strength to carry him without agitating his broken ankle. With all the strength I could muster I placed his arm around my neck and proceeded to carry him along that way. It was hugely unsuccessful. God saw my plight and sent an angel out of nowhere who was witnessing what was taking place. She came along and lifted my son carrying him on her shoulders until we got into the building. I thanked her profusely. Once she left another angel came along out of nowhere with a wheelchair in hand. This enabled me to take him up to the 4th floor by elevator. It was as if I could hear God whisper "I've got you"! Later on that same week the results from the Mayo Clinic came back. It was deemed inconclusive and they too could not diagnose the issue with my liver. So, the decision was made to do surgery on my liver so that treatment for my heart could begin. Surgery was set for December 23rd and the thought of spending Christmas in the hospital made my heart sad. I had already spent my anniversary in the hospital, my birthday sick, and now Christmas was looming. Weeks leading up to the surgery my left arm completely gave out. I could no longer move nor lift my arm. If the arm was bumped, or even if I tried to lay down, the pain emitting from the arm was excruciating. I was forced to see the shoulder surgeon who explained that it would take a full year before the shoulder would rectify itself. So, there I sat dealing with heart issues, ovary issues, liver issues, PTSD issues, a son with a fractured ankle issue, and now a major shoulder issue. I was sinking beyond the weight of it all. The battle continued and I was determined to win this war. According to the Bible, I knew I was already coming from a place of victory, I just needed to start believing it.

Application: Key Verse (Ephesians 6:12), our battle is spiritual not physical. There is a battle that is taking place for our souls that is beyond this world and Satan has enlisted "rulers" and "authorities" to fight this spiritual battle. Since he is the prince of the air and he never stops his attacks, we as Christians must learn to be swordsman/fighters. This means we must constantly be in the word (Bible) and put on God's armor. It will be the ONLY way to counter his attacks and come forth victorious in the *Warfare* taking place all around us. In order to win the war you must be prepared for the battle because evil days will come.

prayer changes things

"For I know the plans I have for you declares the Lord, plans to prosper you and not to harm you, plans to give you hope and a future", Jeremiah 29:11.

The stress had began taking its toll on the household. My husband was trying to keep it together for everyone, my son began banging his head on walls and tables screaming he can't take this anymore, and we then discover that our young daughter was pregnant and brought her home from college. Sometimes amid all the madness you have to stop and smile. I found myself talking to myself and knew I wasn't crazy. The morning of the liver surgery, I became very sick. I felt as if I had a touch of the flu and I was extremely miserable on top of being nervous. The prep nurse advised against having the surgery knowing how sick

I felt but stated that the choice was ultimately mine. My husband, being a teacher, was now home for Christmas break so
the timing was perfect to have someone with me as I would be
recovering at home. Because I was a high-risk patient, I knew
hospital time was inevitable, but the hope was to be home for
Christmas. I made the decision to go ahead with the surgery
despite how I was feeling. Needles were placed in both my
right arm and my left arm. Then an IV was placed in my neck
and I was put to sleep. I awoke to family in my hospital room,
a catheter in my bladder, and terrible pains in my abdomen.
The doctor explained that in his efforts to extract portions of
my liver, he had to remove my gallbladder in the process as
well. No.... not the gallbladder too, I thought! I became so sick
after surgery and was in so much pain that two days later I
still remained in the hospital and it was Christmas Day. I was
eventually released later that day and came home to family
waiting to celebrate my arrival underneath the Christmas tree.
Unfortunately, things took a turn for the worse and two days
later I was back in the hospital due to complications from the
surgery. Sitting was an issue, standing was an issue, walking
was an issue, laying down was an issue and the pain on a scale
from one to ten was a high ten! While in the hospital it didn't
get any better. Since I couldn't bend nor sit, I had to urinate
standing up. To make matters worse, I was unable to have a
bowel movement and it had been over a week. I was impacted
pretty badly. After several days in the hospital I begged to be
discharged. I was in so much discomfort that in my mind if
I were to die let me die at home. With the pain I was experiencing I couldn't see myself out of this predicament no matter
how I forced my mind to conceive it. Thank God for prayer

warriors. These are the individuals you call upon to intercede on your behalf when you are too weak to lift your hands in prayer. From the hospital bed I began to reach out to those individuals that I knew was spending time in God's word and would pray for me. The Lord sent an angel in the form of my mother. Upon my release from the hospital she came to my home and met me there. She spent several weeks by my bedside caring for me, feeding me, and literally teaching me how to walk again.

Application: Key verse (Jeremiah 29:11), it's important to note that God always keeps His covenants. *Prayer Changes Things* and knowing this should be of great encouragement to those that have accepted Christ as their Savior because God does not forsake his children. Since God's response is not always an immediate one, this verse is a reminder that in the middle of hardships and heartaches, God has a promise for the future of his people and this promise involves his plan to prosper them. So, we must trust God and his process which in turn gives us hope.

out of my mind

"Shall we indeed accept good from God, and shall we not accept adversity? In all this Job did not sin with his lips", Job 2:10.

The story is told in the Bible of a man named Job. He was described as an upright man who feared God and rejected evil. The Evil one (Satan) desired to sift him like flour and calamity fell upon his household and struck his body, but the Good one (God) had a plan. The next phase of my journey had me leaning on God like never before. Like Job, I knew I was in the midst of a spiritual warfare and wanted to wave a magic wand to make things better, however, I also realized that the darkest hour is right before dawn and midnight had just begun. My pregnant daughter was now home and experiencing complications with her pregnancy. While my husband was at work during the day, my daughter and I kept each other's company. However, that was short lived as her pregnancy became increasingly problematic. She began bleeding uncontrollably in the later stages of her pregnancy and weekly we were at the Gynecologist office or rushing off to the hospital. This was no way easy on me as I still continued to suffer complications from my illness and heart issues. Seeing the path her pregnancy was taking her, I made the decision to have her baby shower somewhat early in the event the baby came prematurely. Having a shower was a decision I debated with in my mind. She was having the baby out of wedlock and many did not know that she was even pregnant. To add to that there was the stigma of what others would think or even say... especially in the Christian community. After putting it to prayer the Lord whispered in my ears that children are a blessing from Him and gave me a peace to move forward. He also gently reminded me that individuals did not know my daughter's back story regarding her pregnancy and that this too would be a part of her testimony. The shower was a blessing in words that cannot fully be described. Well wishers came and even some that came out of curiosity, however, all that came left knowing the Lord was present and it was good to have been there. My daughter had to leave her own shower early for the hospital. Since she was bleeding the doctor at the hospital made the decision to inject her with steroids in an effort to grow the baby inside her in the event the baby should come early. Several days later we were back to the Gynecologist office as the bleeding continued. We discussed scheduling a planned C-section 4 weeks later to err on the side of caution. We left the Gynecologist's office and stopped at the local Walgreens 10 minutes away to pick up medication the doctor had prescribed. As she stepped out the car to enter the store my daughter looked at me with a troubled look and said "Mom, I'm, peeing on myself". That's when I realized that her water had just broke. I thought to myself, "what are the odds... we JUST left the Gynecologist office". She was scared and I was very nervous. I grabbed the sweater from my car and wrapped it around her to hide her soaked pants. I then escorted her into the restroom at Walgreens while I hastily ran around the store looking for some sanitary napkins to purchase so that she could feel remotely dry while we scrambled to determine our next move. I called the Gynecologist's office and told them that her water had broken. The nurse stated "how.... You just left here less than 10 minutes ago". The doctor called back with the words, "meet me at the hospital, she will need an emergency C-section". The hospital was approximately 10 minutes away from the Walgreens and my home was the same in the opposite direction. I made the split-second decision to head home and pick up my daughter's hospital bag which would give her some time to change into dryer clothes before heading to the hospital. We moved at lighting speed. We grabbed the necessary items and headed straight to the hospital. As we drove, I prayed loudly that the baby wouldn't come in the car and that it would be a complication-free C-section. Nerves filled my daughter and she began to cry. We arrived at the hospital and she was immediately prepped for her surgery. Suddenly it dawned on me that I was alone, scared, and not feeling well. What was supposed to be a joyous occasion felt like a nerve-racking saga. The doctor came out and said, "scrub up, we need you in the delivery room". I was then donned with a scrub suit and mask and whisked away to the operating room. "Lord, I'm so nervous, help me be strong for my daughter" I muttered. The miracle of birth is amazing. I watched my first grandchild leave the womb and enter the world. I thought how life had changed. I was now a grandmother, she was now a mother, and new life had begun. Sadly, the baby was born with a few complications. She was a preemie and her blood sugar levels were extremely low. In addition, they believed she may have contracted an infection and began treating her accordingly. She was placed in the NICU. As my daughter laid in the recovery room and the baby in the NICU I suddenly felt all alone. My husband was at work, my mother was out of town and no one was around to celebrate with me. I called my sister in law in tears and asked if she could come by the hospital and just sit with me. My anxiety began to take over and the palpitations began all over. The week following the baby's birth was a whirlwind. The baby was born on a Tuesday, on Wednesday I was back at the hospital doing a Cardiac Pet Scan on my heart. Once the procedure was completed, I then drove myself to the hospital where my daughter laid to sit by her bedside. Each time she wanted to see her baby she had to be placed in a wheelchair and taken to the NICU. It was a daunting task but one that was necessary. This took place everyday for the next five days. My body was exhausted as my daughter would call me from the hospital to hurry back every day, but I knew she needed me and despite how I was feeling, I held back to be strong for her. On Thursday, while visiting the baby in the NICU I received a call from my cardiologist office with the results from the Pet Scan the previous day. It was not good news. I said nothing to my daughter but simply handed her the baby to hold. Once I left the hospital and got in the parking lot and all I could do was cry. I felt so lonely, I felt as if God had let me down. My mind was shattered and my body was broken. On Friday, my daughter was discharged leaving her baby behind. It was an extremely busy day. She was discharged at 6 *pm* in the evening and I had a function to attend involving my husband at 7 that evening. Although tired, I got my daughter to the car, drove her home from the hospital, unloaded the car and propped her up in the couch downstairs as she was still too weak and sore from her C-section to make it up the stairs. I hurriedly placed a plate of food in front of her with a cell phone and told her I would be back in a hour and a half. I felt extremely guilty leaving her home by herself in her condition, but I also felt the need to support my husband. On my way out I called my neighbor and asked her to check in on my daughter in my absence. I must have called my daughter over a dozen times while at the function just to check in. Once done, I rushed home to tend to her. By midnight, I was fully exhausted. Because the baby was still in the hospital in the NICU and would be there for several weeks, my daughter wanted to make the trip to the hospital everyday to see her baby. This was difficult for several reasons. My body was getting weaker and my daughter was also getting weaker and couldn't walk. Since I had only one arm that was functionable (Frozen Shoulder in the other arm) it was a difficult task to get her in and out of the car, lift her up and push the wheelchair. But in the face of adversity, you will your body to do things that ordinarily you couldn't do. It had been 6 days since the baby was born. It was early evening when we made our way to the NICU to visit the baby. Policy and procedure at the hospital had changed overnight as a new virus call Corona (Covid 19) had just emerged on the scene. As we entered the NICU I could sense that something was wrong. I noticed the nurse whispering and pointing in our direction and I keenly listened with my ears to the conversation at the nurse's station that the head nurse was having on the phone. I heard her mention my granddaughter's name and that the ambulance was in route. I said nothing to my daughter over what I had heard as I didn't want to alarm her unnecessarily. She was already depressed having to leave her newborn in the hospital and I was told to watch for the signs of postpartum on her part. Five minutes into the visit and the head nurse called me to the side. The conversation went a little something like this: "I noticed something unusual while changing your grandbaby and I saved the diaper to show you. It has me extremely concerned. I've been a NICU nurse for over 18 years and I thought it wise to call the doctor in to take a look". My ears perked up and I continued to listen intently. She showed me the diaper and in the baby's stool was blood. She continued "I've also noticed that she's become extremely lethargic over the last 24 hours and she is no longer holding down the formula. Because we are considered a Low Level NICU she will have to be transferred to the Regional hospital that is more equipped to deal with these issues. They are a Level 3 NICU and your grandbaby will be in great hands. The ambulance is presently on it's way to transfer her". My face was stoic. I nodded my head and tried to think of the best way to explain what was happening to my daughter without her having a nervous breakdown. The doctor came in and sat my daughter down. He had a lengthy conversation with her and explained what he thought was happening to our little preemie. I then called my husband and told him what was happening and texted my family to pray. I placed my daughter back into the wheelchair and told the medical attendants that we would meet the ambulance at the Regional hospital. What should have been a 30 minute ride felt like eternity. I was silent, she cried, and the praise and worship music played loudly as we drove. I knew God heard my silent prayer.... but quite honestly, this was too much. We arrived at the hospital and quickly valet the car. Because it was already late in the evening, I was assured by the valet attendant that in the event valet closed the keys would be left at the front desk. I once again placed my daughter in the wheelchair, got processed and cleared from Covid 19 to enter the building, and began pushing the wheelchair to the NICU we had never been to before. It was a daunting task. As I pushed the wheelchair with one arm my body kept telling me I was tired, and my heart felt weak. The Regional hospital is a huge building. I wouldn't doubt that it was over a mile to push the wheelchair from the entrance of the children's hospital to the NICU in the other hospital building. We went from the first floor, to the 4th floor, crossed the bridge and then had to take the elevator down to the 2nd floor before locating the NICU. Next, we had the daunting task of filling out security paperwork and new wrist bands were placed on our arms prior to entering or even walking down the halls of the NICU. Once we got our bearings, we were told were to go to locate the baby. When my eyes laid on her, I held back the tears. Tubes were everywhere, down her tiny nose and down her throat. She had IV's sticking out her little hand and also on her miniature feet. I stood next to my daughter and said nothing. I knew she had to absorb the magnitude of what was happening, and I stood in support. We stood next to the baby's side for couple hours and then out of pure exhaustion realized it was time to go home. We were tired. It had been a long day. Actually, it had been a long week as the last 6 days were relentless. We took the long walk back making our way out of the maze of the hospital with me once again pushing the wheelchair with one hand. Once we made it back to the lobby, we asked for our car keys. We were tired and ready to go home. Searched as he may... the gentleman at the front desk could not find our car keys. He told us to go outside and check to see if the valet driver was still outside. It was dark by now and after 10:00 p.m. and I rolled my daughter's wheelchair outside and saw no one except another gentleman in plain clothing sitting as if waiting for his ride. We attempted to ask him if he had seen the valet driver but he didn't respond, and so we sat next to him as we waited for the front desk personnel to figure out where the valet driver was and what he had done with our car keys. An hour went by and we were no closer to an answer regarding our vehicle. I wanted for this day to be over and it seemed as if a new adventure had just begun late at night. Frustrated as we were the front desk personnel came outside where we sat all dumbfounded trying to assess what our next move would be. Myself, my daughter, the gentleman waiting for his ride, and the hospital employee struck up a conversation on the bench. That's when we discovered that the gentleman waiting for his ride only spoke Spanish, and he was also the valet driver the entire time that we were looking for. He sat hearing our entire conversation, but because he spoke no English, he hadn't a clue that he was the missing link. If it weren't for the front desk personnel who spoke Spanish and was able to figure out that this was the valet driver two minutes into our conversation on the bench, we might all still be sitting there to this very day. I didn't know whether to scream or laugh. My daughter and I looked at each other in total disbelief. We then gave the valet attendant the ticket to our car and had the front desk personal translate and tell him our car was a Honda, Pilot. He would have no problem finding our vehicle as it was probably the only car still left in the parking garage. The valet driver left to retrieve the car and we sat on the bench laughing waiting patiently for his return. A half hour went by.... No valet driver. An hour went by.... No valet driver. Suddenly he appeared on foot, sweating like a wildebeest with no car. This could NOT be happening. "Where's my car", I asked. I was too tired to yell. I noticed that he and the front desk personal with voices raised dialogued between each other in Spanish before I was told "He can't find your car". I paused, took a deep breath, and asked the Lord NOT to let the "angry, black woman" come out. We spoke amongst ourselves, me to the hospital worker, and the hospital worker to the valet driver. We discovered that although he was told the vehicle was a Honda Pilot, he was looking for a Toyota. As I threw my arms in the air in disbelief I watched as the front desk attendant took my valet ticket out of the hands of the valet driver. As he did so he flipped the ticket on the other side to discover a written note stating where the car had been parked. Because the valet driver couldn't speak nor read English, he had no idea what it said. He had been searching for the car in the wrong parking garage. I looked around searching for the hidden camera. Was I being punked? This was unprecedented. By now it was midnight and we still didn't have our vehicle. The valet driver set out once again on foot this time driving back in a

=GRACE!!

Honda Pilot, our Honda Pilot. I gently placed my daughter in the car, tipped the front desk personal and began the drive home. We got home after 1:00 a.m. and I couldn't be any happier to see my bed.

Application: Key verse (Job 2:10), It is so easy to accept the good in life and when bad enters blame God. Has the thought ever entered that maybe God was not the responsible party or is the thought that he could have prevented it since he is God! Regardless of your thoughts, it's important to note that even in the adversity moments God still sits on the throne. So, when God allows adversity, bridle your tongue. We may feel like God is not treating us fairly but trust the process. His grace is sufficient in the midst of trials and tribulations even when you are going *Out of your Mind*. Feel free to ask God questions but don't question His authority allowing your feelings to rule your response.

new beginnings

"He giveth power to the faint; and to them that have no might He increaseth strength", Isaiah 40:29.

The next day after our saga the night before my daughter woke up complaining that she was in excruciating pain. Her ability to walk had gotten worse and I could tell that something was not right. She begged to be taken to the Emergency Room and that's when I knew that she wasn't well. My mother was flying into town from being away on vacation to not only see her new great grand but to assist me as well. I loaded my daughter into the car and expressed to her that I needed to pick up her grandmother from the airport and then would immediately take her to the Emergency Room. Driving for me especially with my heart condition was still not easy. It was a battle of my mind each time I got behind the wheel to will myself into actually driving. Too many "what if's" would flood my thoughts but I had no other choice. With my daughter in tote I picked my mother up from the airport and headed straight for the Emergency Room. Since she couldn't walk, we needed assistance at the hospital to get her out of the car. The new treat of the Corona virus didn't make things any easier. Just getting into the Emergency Room was like trying to break into a Federal building. The Emergency room was flooded with people and we sat and waited.... and waited and waited some more. After what seemed like eternity, she was finally called in. After spending the entire day in the Emergency Room she was diagnosed with what was believed to be a pinched nerve or Sciatica in her lower back. By the time of her discharge it was already 7 p.m. We had spent 9 hours in the ER. She was then loaded back onto a wheelchair and we began to make our way upstairs in the hospital to visit the baby in the NICU. The sheer gleam on my mother's face seeing her great grandchild for the first time made us all smile after a long day. By the time we got home it was extremely late. Another day in the record books. My mom's visit was short lived. She began to feel sick and thought it best to go home. Since the Corona virus was beginning to make a name for itself in the U.S., we thought it best for her to quarantine herself at her home until she was feeling better. She jumped into her car and left the very next day. As for my daughter, her health went from bad to worse almost overnight. Her inability to walk became even weaker and she could no longer stand on her own. She began urinating all over herself and even had to be hand washed. Since my husband was at work it became my task to lift her out of the bed with one hand and muster the strength to take her to the bathroom and tend to her needs. This was so difficult as I could tell my body was weakening under the pressure of it all. To make matters even worse, she had the desire to see her baby in the NICU and it was an arduous task lifting her into the car and wheeling her back and forth to the hospital in her debilitating condition. Most days I sat and cried because I was broken. Things just kept falling apart and I felt stifled. Eventually, a family member who was a part of the medical community took notice of what was occurring. She came by the home and when she saw the condition of my daughter and myself, she immediately loaded my daughter into the car and took her back to the hospital. My daughter was admitted and spent several days in the hospital as they tried to diagnose what was really happening to her. It was the belief of some that her epidural at the time of her C-section had gone horribly wrong and that her inability to walk and the excruciating pain she was feeling was a result of that. No one in the medical community wanted to take responsibility for it and each person kept blaming someone else. My husband and I sat at home.... Stuck! Our daughter was at one hospital and our grand daughter was at another hospital. Due to the threat of the Corona virus (Covid 19) we were unable to see either one of them. We even tried explaining to the supervisor in the NICU that the baby's mother was ill and in the hospital, however, they still would not allow us both to see the baby. After five days in the hospital my daughter was discharged but left in a worse condition than when she entered. She had now lost ALL mobility to walk and could no longer stand. She was being discharged with an IV that had to be administered at home and health care services. The family member that previously had whisked her away to the hospital stepped in and took her into her home so that my body could get the rest it needed. So, for one week after her discharge my daughter lived with another family member. Quite honestly, I felt like a failure of a mother, but I knew it was the best thing for both of us at the time. Amid all this chaos, my cardiologist called to say that I would have to begin my new round of treatment for my heart. The medications would be heavy and the side effects even worse, but it was necessary in order to treat the inflammation in my heart and reduce the discomfort I continued to feel. The treatment would last for 3 months and in the 4th month they would retest me to see if any improvements were shown. "Lord, are you there? Are you here in my darkness" was my cry! I had NOTHING left to give. The week following her discharge from the hospital, we received a call from the NICU that our little preemie was doing so much better, that the IV's and the tubes had been removed and she was ready to go home. What an answer to prayers. My husband and I drove to the home where our daughter was staying, loaded her and her belongings into the car, and headed straight to the hospital to retrieve the baby. After 3 weeks in the NICU, our granddaughter and our daughter were both finally coming home. A new normal had begun. Since my daughter was unable to walk, she was forced to sleep downstairs on the couch. Our home was two story's without a bedroom on the first floor. If her baby cried, she was unable to stand and retrieve her baby. It was a sad sight to behold. In an effort to assist, we placed the bassinet next to the couch where she slept so all she had to do was reach over and touch the baby. Unfortunately, she was also unable to bend to lift the baby and required help to do so. It was a sad sight to behold! Over the next month my daughter had the audios task of administering medication to her picc line twice a day from home. She needed physical therapy but was unable to make it out the home nor have individuals in the home due to the heighten risk of Covid 19. My husband and I took it upon ourselves to conduct a make shift PT (physical therapy) at home for her. She eventually began to learn the basics all over again. She learned how to stand on her own, and eventually with the assistance of a Walker learned to begin taking steps once again. We celebrated a month later when she was finally off her picc line and was able to walk, albeit slowly, without the walker. Our greatest joy came from seeing her holding her baby without the need for assistance. Our God is always on time.

Application: Key verse (Isaiah 40:29), Our God is always on time. Let that resonate for a moment. He's never late nor does He come too early, but He is timely. In those moments when your faith becomes weak, that's when His grace is the strongest... why, because he increases your strength. The power he possess, he freely gives to the weary. Sometimes we don't experience this power because we fail to ask for it. Remember, those who trust in their own strength will fail no matter how capable they may appear to be. *New Beginnings* start with a fresh perspective from God.

the next chapter

"See, I have refined you, though not as silver, I have tested you in the furnace of affliction", Isaiah 48:10

How do you find beauty in something that has been so marked? When life changes in an instant and all you see are the ruins and you dig deep to find peace in the midst of the storm. The Bible says, *"Be still and know that I am God", Psalm 46:10*, and it's in the stillness that you hear His voice. If you aren't careful, you may miss it. But you must be in relationship with Him to know His voice when He speaks. You won't be aware of His presence if you haven't been spending time in His presence. It is there that you will find beauty in the ashes. As my treatment plan winds down, the medications have taken a toll on my internal organs. My kidneys are spilling protein, my blood sugar levels are now elevated, my liver enzymes are elevated, my cholesterol is elevated, my hair is falling out, and the steroids have caused my weight to balloon 30 pounds heavier and my face to become twisted. There is a battle that continues to take place in my mind, but I've learned that God's grace is sufficient because it sustains. God never promised to take all our trials away but He has promised that He would be with us in the midst of the storm *("The Lord your God goes with you; he will never leave you nor forsake you", Deuteronomy 31:6).* As I reflect on my health challenges, especially over the last 18 months I continue to marvel at His faithfulness. I should have been dead a long time ago. Many might ask or even conclude "Why do you continue to serve a God who allows bad things to happen to seemingly good people"? I ask.... "Should I only take good from God and when faced with adversity, curse Him"? This is a testing of my faith and I know that regardless of my circumstances, I've already won! Where there is good, there is also evil. Sometimes we blame God for something the Devil has committed. Stay focused! Faith is defined in the Bible as *"The substance of things hoped for, the evidence of things not seen", Hebrews 11:1.* Since my relationship with the Lord is based on faith, I take Him completely at His word as I believe His words are true. Spiritual warfare is real. If you haven't yet experienced it, your time will come. How will you respond? Will you curse God or trust Him in your storm? There is peace in His presence when you remain still long enough to find the beauty from the ashes. My story continues to be written......

"The spirit of the Lord God is upon me, because the Lord has anointed me to bring good new to the suffering and afflicted. He has sent me to comfort the broken hearted, to announce

liberty to captives and to open the eyes of the blind. He has sent me to tell those who mourn that the time of God's favor to them has come, and the day of his wrath to their enemies. To all who mourn in Israel he will give: beauty for ashes, joy instead of mourning; praise instead of heaviness. For God has planted them like strong and graceful oaks for his own glory", Isaiah 61: 1-3.

Support

*Don't do life alone (reach out)
*Seek help (get counseling if needed)
*Read the Bible (it has helped millions)
*Pray (it changes things)
*Accept Christ (and watch the results)

Connect with me on Facebook @ Defibrillator Buddies.
Let's talk, you are not alone!

** "Defibrillator Buddies" is a support group created by myself for individuals who have had anxieties triggered by a Defibrillator implant.**

epilogue

I have been changed.... Scars will do that to you! But they are permanent reminders of something past. My journey didn't stop and sometimes you have to hit rock bottom before climbing up. You learn a lot in the valley. You learn who your friends are, you certainly learn how to pray, and if you don't have a spiritual compass it bends you into believing in something or better yet someone. The valley can be a dark place. After my body began "shutting down" the side effects from the medications began wreaking havoc on my already weaken immune system. My feet felt like there were on pins and needles, I couldn't walk for any extended period of time, as a result. The heavy steroids gave my face the swollen, moonlike effect, my weight ballooned, I began seeing flashes in my eyes and my vision began to deteriorate. If that wasn't enough, I developed kidney stones and a UTI with a bad strand of E-Coli that 3 months of continuous antibiotics could not heal. I was in the valley. At this point I had so many doctor's appointments and lab work that I lost count and my veins began forming tracks on my now sore hands from so many needles. It got to the point where 13 vials of blood for lab work was the norm and they either could no longer find my veins or I had to be stuck numerous times. To add insult to injury whenever they were able to find a vein the blood flow would cease and I would have to be stuck all over again. I begged my cardiologist to take me off these heavy meds but she begged me to see it through several more months. Another cardiac pet scan showed that there was no improvement to my heart. It was at this point my doctor, with compassion in her eyes, said "I'm so sorry for you". What a witnessing opportunity I thought.... I told her my story was still being written. My cardiologist agreed to do paperwork to get me to the Mayo Clinic. I was grateful but knew that Mayo would not see me as I had reached out several months earlier, but they stated that they did not take my health insurance. What I needed was a miracle from God. My cardiologist gave me over temporarily to another local doctor who dealt with auto immune issues in hopes that they would be able to assist me with my medications. They ordered more blood work and my heart literally sunk once again. While waiting for the blood results to come back I received a call from my Oncologist stating that I would need to repeat my liver MRI. I wanted to scream. This meant back to the hospital.

> **"For the mountains may be removed and the hills may shake, But My lovingkindness will not be removed from you, And My covenant of peace will not be shaken," says the Lord who has compassion on you (Isaiah 54:10)**

The dictionary defines a Valley as an "elongated depression between uplands, hills or mountains, especially one following the course of a stream". In the Bible, the "valley" is usually described as "a place or rest, or time of joy, between the mountains". What a contrast. I was especially struck by the word DEPRESSION in the definition. I was in a state of depression in the valley. It was not a time of joy for me and I was certainly restless. As I awaited my MRI, the Lord lead me to have a conversation with my daughter. She was open, honest, and upfront and the situation was worse than I expected. As mentioned in the chapter entitled "Seasons" somethings are too difficult to speak. I had reached my breaking point. I needed a breakthrough. Several weeks later as my family and I sat watching the news we received a call that my husband's brother was found dead in his home. Within the weeks that followed we received more sad news of additional friends and relatives making the transition from this life into the next. Within a month's span we lost at least 11 close friends. Due to a pandemic, we were unable to attend their funerals. At this point I longed for the valley that the Bible spoke of. I wanted to drink from the stream and find joy between the mountains. Then I received a breakthrough my spirit needed to hear. The auto immune doctor called to say that my blood work showed (and I quote) "you are the healthiest, unhealthy person we know". Translation.... Your bloodwork is PERFECT! Later that week, I received a call from my Oncologist stating that the liver MRI was fine. For the first time in months, I felt like I could BREATHEEE!!! There was still this major issue with my heart which was unresolved. In desperation I picked up the phone and dialed the number to the Mayo Clinic. I'm not sure what I expected as I had been denied in the past due to my health insurance. Then I heard these words that still resonates to this very day "yes, we take your insurance"! I had reached my mountain top.

As fate would have it a turn of events took place after my mountain top experience. I began to notice blood in my stool. I contacted the gastroenterologist who scheduled a colonoscopy. After giving my health information to the receptionist on the phone my colonoscopy was scheduled in an out patient facility. The prep was horrible. I had fluid coming through both sides of my body and could hold nothing down. It was concerning enough for me to consider a trip to the hospital, but at the heights of Covid I was apprehensive about stepping foot into a hospital so I suffered at home with the thought of "this will soon be over" ringing in my head. The next day my husband took me to the facility for my procedure. As I was being prepped on the gurney, a conversation ensued with the nurse in charge of my care. I told her about my experience the night before and she was a bit concerned as to whether my body was cleared enough to proceed with the procedure. She sent me back to the restroom and still had her doubts. An hour or so had passed and I was still on the gurney awaiting my procedure. She approached me and stated that she wanted to make sure I was clear in the colon and so she had me to get dressed and gave me more solution to drink. "Take this bottle" she stated, "Go home for about two hours and drink the liquid in this bottle. Come back and we will proceed". I was upset but got dressed, called my husband and told him to pick me up and all that had transpired. At home the vomiting started all over again. The cramping in my stomach was unbearable but I kept telling myself to push through. Two hours later, I was back at the facility, barely able to walk. I

was prepped all over again. The IV was inserted and as I awaited being issued into the surgical room for my procedure, another conversation took place with the nurse. We began talking
about the fact that she was a former ICU nurse in the heart
ward. I started sharing with her my heart history. There was
a big pause and she went to get the doctor. As I laid there, my
gut knew something wasn't right. I watched as they whispered
in the corner amongst themselves. The doctor called the on-
site cardiologist name. He asked for my cardiologist name. "We
need to make a call" they stated. Moments later they returned.
"I'm so sorry, we cannot continue with this procedure. It must
be done at a hospital". I wanted to scream, yell, shout! Who
dropped the ball, I thought. They knew my medical history as it
was shared in length prior to the procedure being scheduled....
and now THIS! I was beside myself. They took the IV out of my
arm, told me to get dressed, and apologized profusely. I felt so
defeated once more. With tears streaming down my face God
quietly reminded me "You are more than a conqueror".

And just like that, my many trips to the Mayo Clinic began.
From my home it was roughly a five hour drive and due to the
nature of some of my appointments they required over night
stay. This meant besides the cost of gas to travel, the cost of
hotel, food, and medical expenses were astronomical especially
for someone who wasn't working. Since I required additional attention, my husband made the dauting decision to take a Leave
from his job to tend to our household. That meant zero income
to our household. With school being online (due to Covid) we
had to shuffle our son back and forth with us each time we trav-
eled. He began missing classes during the hours we were on
the road. This was becoming too much. I distinctly remember

one set of appointments at Mayo which required several days of arduous testing. It was during this time that I noticed something different was occurring with my body. My stomach felt nauseous, and I had severe cramping with diarrhea. As I sat there in the hotel room it dawned on me that this diarrhea had been occurring every day for several weeks. I tried hard to convince myself that maybe I had a nervous stomach due to all the testing I was enduring at the Mayo Clinic, but truth be told, I knew something was wrong. During one particular test as the nurse prepared the IV in my arm, I tried to explain to her the selective nature of my veins. I begged her to use a "butterfly" needle, knowing my veins were problematic but she stated that this particular test needed a big needle. "Hold back the tears" I told myself... "don't cry"! I KNEW this meant being stuck several times. I tried to tell her that they would have a difficult time finding my veins, but of course, I wasn't believed. That would be insulting the nurse over my care who has stuck many veins in her career but I knew what was to come. Many unsuccessful sticks and apologies later she was forced to call in the ultrasound technician to try and locate my veins using the ultrasound machine. After wiping my tears which were flowing by this time, the needle was finally inserted. Once the test for that day was completed I begged the nurses to allow me to keep the IV in my arm as the following days test would require more needles and I didn't want to go through another debacle like the one I had just experienced. They agreed and wrapped my hand tightly so that the needle wouldn't move. To say that everything went as planned just wouldn't be my "Job" story. As you may recall in the chapter entitled "Out of my Mind", the character from the Bible (Job) experienced things that humanly speaking would cause the average human to fold. That night, I was in excruciating pain from the needle. I could not move my arm and the slightest motion would send me over the edge. Between the pain from the needle in my arm and running to the bathroom every 10 minutes from this continuous diarrhea, it made for one awful night. The next day, once all my testing was completed and the IV was removed, my arm remained swollen where the needle once was. I was simply glad to be on my way home with days of testing behind me but with the worry of something just isn't right with my stomach.

Enter colonoscopy number two, this time scheduled at the hospital. Shortly after my last trip to the Mayo Clinic, I called my gastroenterologist with worry in my voice making him aware that I had diarrhea continuously for one month every day without relief. I was holding nothing in. It was scary and my mind began going places I didn't want it to tread. The stomach cramping and diarrhea had become so bad that I was forced to travel with my grand baby's diaper in my purse in the event I should have an "accident". Humbling......! Then just like my last experience the prep for my colonoscopy was horrible. I was vomiting every ounce of the liquid given, screaming out in excruciating pain as my stomach doubled over in camps that no man, woman, or child should ever have to experience. It didn't help the scenario that the diarrhea didn't stop. I just wanted it to be all over, déjà vu! The next day my husband took me to the hospital and my second colonoscopy was on its way. They were able to get the needle in with one stick and I began to smile until the attending nurse asked, "is your stool clear". I was not about to go through what I had experienced a month earlier. I softly told her that I had vomited up the prep but due to a month's worth of diarrhea I thought I would be clear enough to proceed. After the procedure was completed, the doctor came in my room with the news that I had a severe infection in my colon (thus all the diarrhea, cramping and blood in my stool), they found several polyps and that I would have to repeat my colonoscopy since I wasn't cleared enough. In my mind I REFUSED to go back through another procedure, but that too would be short lived. After leaving the hospital, my husband drove to the pharmacy to pick up the antibiotics needed for my infection. I was warned that they were heavy antibiotics and the side effects would be brutal, but for the next 10 days purpose to stay the course. I came home, laid in my bed and attempted to rest. The next day in an attempt to lift my spirits, I jumped in the shower to wash my hair. As the water ran over my skin, I knew something was array. My body began to feel very itchy. I tried to dismiss it as the shampoo and water ran through my scalp but my mind said, "something isn't right". I quickly jumped out the shower and began drying myself off. The first thing I noticed as I looked in the mirror was that my hair was completely matted. It wasn't tangled, but matted from the root to the ends of my hair. This had never happened before in my entire life. As I glanced at my hair in the mirror I noticed my face was swelling up before my eyes. I looked down on my naked body and saw hives popping up on my skin, down my arms, torso, and legs. I immediately knew, I was having an allergic reaction. I didn't know what was causing it. I had done nothing different than I had done in all my years of living but something was array. I ran out the bathroom to my husband and said "honey, I'm on fire. My body is burning all over and I'm itchy". I saw the look on his face and it spelled…. Panic! We immediately began rummaging through the house for some Benadryl. Although old and expired I popped several in my mouth in hopes that it would minimize the swelling and the hives. Within 15 minutes the itching began to subside and the body burning eased. I began to cry all over again. My spirit was crushed and I was a ball of mess. Later that evening we began to tackle my matted hair. But it was useless, the hair would not budge. We Googled every hair remedy under the sun from vinegar to homemade conditioners. By now it was three o'clock in the morning and we both sat looking defeated. The hives were still on my body and my hair resembled a matted dog and NO remedies were working. I resigned for the night in hopes of a better morning. It was not to be. The next day I willed myself out of the bed and slowly wondered if the last several days, weeks, months, year, had been an awful dream... a night terror! I was apprehensive to eat anything as I was still suffering from my colon infection and had fears of another, out of the blue, allergic reaction. For breakfast and throughout the day I kept it simple, tea and dry crackers. I then went back upstairs to figure out the next move with my hair. That's when I noticed I was feeling itchy all over again. I looked down on my arm and saw hives appearing before my eyes. I looked at my face and saw swelling and hives. Down my neck and torso as if something out of a horror movie my body began giving way. I began screaming for my husband to come into the room. Another severe allergic reaction. More Benadryl and thoughts of going to the hospital with Covid raging. I looked at myself in the mirror and for a brief moment I didn't recognize the face looking back. My hair was matted, my body was under attack, my eyes were red and swollen from crying and black circles covered my eyes. I sat in my ash cloth on the toilet seat and bawled. *"The Lord is near to the broken-hearted and saves the crushed in spirit" Psalm 34:18.*

I made the dauting decision to shave down my hair.... not because I wanted to but I had no other choice. They say the hair is a woman's glory, well my magnificence was gone! I called my hair dresser and told her I was in desperation and needed to come in. As I sat in her chair watching my locs fall to the ground I bit my tongue to hold back the tears. When she was done I was silent looking in the mirror. I felt ugly, dejected, empty, and overall wasted. I suddenly had a new found respect for Cancer patients. It was humbling. It was at this very moment I heard the Lord's voice. It was clear and it was firm. "New Beginnings", He said. The previous year in all my turmoil His words were "Be Thankful". I struggled with those words in my darkest of times yet, it was those same words that kept me sane. He was constantly reminding me to be more aware of His presence. And now.... "New Beginnings"! My husband picked me up and didn't say a word. Men can be funny at times, but his silence spoke volumes. He didn't recognize me either.

So here I sit, awaiting my 3rd colonoscopy in 4 months. I am now riddled in pain from osteoarthritis which has suddenly come upon me. To tell you all of which I have experienced in recent months would be to bear my soul wide open. I've only tipped the iceberg. I most recently took my first walk around the block of my home by myself. It was liberating. In my head I have goals I desire to accomplish. Two steps forward and three steps back and then a giant leap. God softly reminds me that His mercies are new EVERYDAY. So, I ask him to take captive my thoughts and that they would yield to Him. I purpose not to live in the past, nor to worry about the future, but to revel in the dawning of a new day... today! *"The steadfast love of the Lord never ceases, his mercies never come to an end; they are new every morning; great is your faithfulness" (Lamentations 3:22-23)*. Always know that beauty can be found in the ashes because there is peace in the midst of the storm when you walk with Jesus.

acknowledgments

To all who prayed, visited, sent cards, sat by my bedside, brought meals, encouraged, drove me to my many doctor's visits, called, sent text messages, wiped my tears, and simply did life with me, words cannot fully express my gratitude. I salute and thank you!